# TEACHER'S PET PUBLICATIONS

PUZZLE PACK
for
Holes

based on the book by
Louis Sachar

Written by
William T. Collins

© 2005 Teacher's Pet Publications
All Rights Reserved

The materials in this packet are copyrighted
by Teacher's Pet Publications, Inc.

These pages may be duplicated by the purchaser
for use in the purchaser's own classroom.

Copying any of these materials and distributing them
for any other purpose is a violation of the copyright laws.

© 2005 Teacher's Pet Publications, Inc.
www.tpet.com

INTRODUCTION
If you already own the LitPlan for this title, this Puzzle Pack will refresh your Unit Resource Materials and Vocabulary Resource Materials sections plus give you additional materials you can substitute into the tests. If you do not already have a complete LitPlan, these pages will give you some supplemental materials to use with your own plan. There are two main groups of materials: one set for unit words (such as characters' names, symbols, places, etc.) and one set for vocabulary words associated with the book.

WORD LIST
There is a word list for both the unit words and the vocabulary words. These lists show you which words are being used in the materials and the clues or definitions being used for those words. You may want to give students a word list with clues/definitions to help them, or you may want students to only have a word list (without clues/definitions) if you want them to work a little harder. Both are available for duplication. The word lists can also be your "calling key" for the bingo games.

FILL IN THE BLANK AND MATCHING
There are 4 each of the fill in the blank and matching worksheets for both the unit and vocabulary words. These pages can be used either as extra worksheets for students or as objective parts of a unit test. They can be done individually if students need extra help or as a whole class activity to review the material covered.

MAGIC SQUARES
The magic squares not only reinforce the material covered but also work on reasoning and math skills. Many teachers have told us that their students really enjoy doing these!

WORD SEARCH PUZZLES
The word search words go in all directions, as indicated on your answer keys. Two of the word search puzzles have the clues listed rather than the words. This makes the puzzle a little more difficult, but it reinforces the material better. Two word search puzzles have words only for students who find the clue puzzles too difficult.

CROSSWORD PUZZLES
Both unit and vocabulary word sections have 4 crossword puzzles.

BINGO CARDS
There are 32 individual bingo cards for the unit words and 32 individual bingo cards for the vocabulary words. You can use your word list as a "call list," calling the words at random and marking them off of your list as you go, or you could use the flash cards by cutting them apart and drawing the words at random from a hat (or box or whatever). To make a better review, you might ask for the definition and spelling of each word as you call it out–or you could call out the definitions and have students tell you the words they need to look for on the puzzle.

JUGGLE LETTERS
The vocabulary juggle letter game is intended to help students learn the spellings of the words. One sheet has the definitions listed on it as an extra help for students who need it or to reinforce the definitions if you choose to do so.

FLASH CARDS
We've included a set of vocabulary flash cards you can duplicate, cut, and fold for your students. Some teachers make a few sets for general use by the class; others make a set for each student. Some teachers duplicate them for each student and have the students cut & fold their own. You can cut out just the words and put them in a hat, have each student pick out one word and write the definition and a sentence for that word. Students then swap words and papers, with the next student adding a sentence of his own under the last one. You can have students swap as many times as you like. Each time the student will read the sentences written prior to his own and then add a sentence. You can cut out the words and definitions separately and play "I Have; Who Has?" Each student in the room draws a word and definition. The first student says, "I have (the name of the word). Who has the definition?" The student with the definition reads it then says, "I have (the name of the vocabulary word she has). Who has the definition?" The round continues until all words and definitions have been given.

Holes Word List

No.	Word	Clue/Definition
1.	BARLOW	Katherine's last name
2.	BASEBALL	Game Clyde Livingston played
3.	BOAT	Zero hid under it.
4.	CAVEMAN	Stanley's nickname
5.	DONKEY	Original Mary Lou was Sam's ___.
6.	ELYA	Stanley's great-great-grandfather
7.	FEET	Sweet ___; Clyde's nickname
8.	GREEN	Camp ___ Lake
9.	GYPSY	A one-legged one put a curse on the family
10.	HECTOR	Zero's real name
11.	HOLES	Title of the book
12.	JEWELS	These were in the suitcase Stanley & Zero found.
13.	LAUGHING	Miss Barlow was doing this when she died.
14.	LIPSTICK	Stanley found a ___ tube in the hole he dug.
15.	LIZARDS	Dangerous, yellow-spotted ones inhabited the area.
16.	LOU	Sam's boat: Mary ___
17.	MOM	Mr. Pendanski's nickname
18.	ONIONS	Sam offered these as a remedy.
19.	ONLY	Lullaby: If ___; if ___.
20.	PEACHES	Katherine made these.
21.	PENDANSKI	Name of the counselor
22.	READ	What Zero could not do
23.	RED	Color of Warden's hair and nails
24.	SACHAR	Author
25.	SEEDS	Mr. Sir ate sunflower ___.
26.	SHOVEL	Digging utensil
27.	SIR	He referred to a Girl Scout camp: Mr. ___
28.	SPAT	What each boy did when he finished digging his hole
29.	SPLOOSH	Zero drank it.
30.	TEACHER	Katherine Barlow's original profession
31.	THUMBS	Signal Stanley & Zero gave: ___ up
32.	VENOM	Ingredient in Warden's nail polish
33.	WARDEN	Woman who ran the camp
34.	WATER	Kind of truck Stanley stole and wrecked
35.	WRECK	Sign on the rec room door: ____ Room
36.	YELNATS	Stanley's last name
37.	ZERO	He escaped from the camp before Stanley did.
38.	ZERONI	Madame who was a one-legged Gypsy
39.	ZIGZAG	Zero attacked him when he started to beat Stanley.

Copyrighted

Holes Fill In The Blanks 1

_____ 1. Author
_____ 2. Katherine's last name
_____ 3. Sam offered these as a remedy.
_____ 4. What each boy did when he finished digging his hole
_____ 5. Sam's boat: Mary ___
_____ 6. Color of Warden's hair and nails
_____ 7. A one-legged one put a curse on the family
_____ 8. Camp ___ Lake
_____ 9. Name of the counselor
_____ 10. Digging utensil
_____ 11. Stanley found a ___ tube in the hole he dug.
_____ 12. He escaped from the camp before Stanley did.
_____ 13. Katherine made these.
_____ 14. Title of the book
_____ 15. Stanley's great-great-grandfather
_____ 16. Zero drank it.
_____ 17. Mr. Sir ate sunflower ___.
_____ 18. Lullaby: If ___; if ___.
_____ 19. Original Mary Lou was Sam's ___.
_____ 20. What Zero could not do

Holes Fill In The Blanks 1 Answer Key

SACHAR	1. Author
BARLOW	2. Katherine's last name
ONIONS	3. Sam offered these as a remedy.
SPAT	4. What each boy did when he finished digging his hole
LOU	5. Sam's boat: Mary ___
RED	6. Color of Warden's hair and nails
GYPSY	7. A one-legged one put a curse on the family
GREEN	8. Camp ___ Lake
PENDANSKI	9. Name of the counselor
SHOVEL	10. Digging utensil
LIPSTICK	11. Stanley found a ___ tube in the hole he dug.
ZERO	12. He escaped from the camp before Stanley did.
PEACHES	13. Katherine made these.
HOLES	14. Title of the book
ELYA	15. Stanley's great-great-grandfather
SPLOOSH	16. Zero drank it.
SEEDS	17. Mr. Sir ate sunflower ___.
ONLY	18. Lullaby: If ___; if ___.
DONKEY	19. Original Mary Lou was Sam's ___.
READ	20. What Zero could not do

Holes Fill In The Blanks 2

_____

1. Camp ___ Lake
2. Katherine Barlow's original profession
3. Stanley's great-great-grandfather
4. Miss Barlow was doing this when she died.
5. Zero's real name
6. What each boy did when he finished digging his hole
7. Mr. Sir ate sunflower ___.
8. A one-legged one put a curse on the family
9. Game Clyde Livingston played
10. Sam offered these as a remedy.
11. Sign on the rec room door: ____ Room
12. Zero drank it.
13. Signal Stanley & Zero gave: ___ up
14. Author
15. Title of the book
16. Stanley's nickname
17. These were in the suitcase Stanley & Zero found.
18. Original Mary Lou was Sam's ___.
19. Mr. Pendanski's nickname
20. He referred to a Girl Scout camp: Mr. ___

Holes Fill In The Blanks 2 Answer Key

GREEN	1.	Camp ___ Lake
TEACHER	2.	Katherine Barlow's original profession
ELYA	3.	Stanley's great-great-grandfather
LAUGHING	4.	Miss Barlow was doing this when she died.
HECTOR	5.	Zero's real name
SPAT	6.	What each boy did when he finished digging his hole
SEEDS	7.	Mr. Sir ate sunflower ___.
GYPSY	8.	A one-legged one put a curse on the family
BASEBALL	9.	Game Clyde Livingston played
ONIONS	10.	Sam offered these as a remedy.
WRECK	11.	Sign on the rec room door: ____ Room
SPLOOSH	12.	Zero drank it.
THUMBS	13.	Signal Stanley & Zero gave: ___ up
SACHAR	14.	Author
HOLES	15.	Title of the book
CAVEMAN	16.	Stanley's nickname
JEWELS	17.	These were in the suitcase Stanley & Zero found.
DONKEY	18.	Original Mary Lou was Sam's ___.
MOM	19.	Mr. Pendanski's nickname
SIR	20.	He referred to a Girl Scout camp: Mr. ___

Holes Fill In The Blanks 3

_____

1. Mr. Sir ate sunflower ___.
2. Mr. Pendanski's nickname
3. Signal Stanley & Zero gave: ___ up
4. Zero's real name
5. Katherine made these.
6. Camp ___ Lake
7. Woman who ran the camp
8. He referred to a Girl Scout camp: Mr. ___
9. Stanley found a ___ tube in the hole he dug.
10. Author
11. Sam's boat: Mary ___
12. What Zero could not do
13. Digging utensil
14. Kind of truck Stanley stole and wrecked
15. Game Clyde Livingston played
16. Lullaby: If ___; if ___.
17. Katherine Barlow's original profession
18. Sam offered these as a remedy.
19. Dangerous, yellow-spotted ones inhabited the area.
20. What each boy did when he finished digging his hole

Holes Fill In The Blanks 3 Answer Key

SEEDS	1. Mr. Sir ate sunflower ___.
MOM	2. Mr. Pendanski's nickname
THUMBS	3. Signal Stanley & Zero gave: ___ up
HECTOR	4. Zero's real name
PEACHES	5. Katherine made these.
GREEN	6. Camp ___ Lake
WARDEN	7. Woman who ran the camp
SIR	8. He referred to a Girl Scout camp: Mr. ___
LIPSTICK	9. Stanley found a ___ tube in the hole he dug.
SACHAR	10. Author
LOU	11. Sam's boat: Mary ___
READ	12. What Zero could not do
SHOVEL	13. Digging utensil
WATER	14. Kind of truck Stanley stole and wrecked
BASEBALL	15. Game Clyde Livingston played
ONLY	16. Lullaby: If ___; if ___.
TEACHER	17. Katherine Barlow's original profession
ONIONS	18. Sam offered these as a remedy.
LIZARDS	19. Dangerous, yellow-spotted ones inhabited the area.
SPAT	20. What each boy did when he finished digging his hole

Holes Fill In The Blanks 4

1. Zero drank it.
2. Sweet ___; Clyde's nickname
3. Miss Barlow was doing this when she died.
4. Color of Warden's hair and nails
5. Lullaby: If ___; if ___.
6. Woman who ran the camp
7. Signal Stanley & Zero gave: ___ up
8. Title of the book
9. Katherine made these.
10. Zero hid under it.
11. Zero's real name
12. He escaped from the camp before Stanley did.
13. Original Mary Lou was Sam's ___.
14. What each boy did when he finished digging his hole
15. Mr. Sir ate sunflower ___.
16. Sign on the rec room door: ____ Room
17. Name of the counselor
18. Katherine Barlow's original profession
19. Camp ___ Lake
20. Ingredient in Warden's nail polish

Holes Fill In The Blanks 4 Answer Key

SPLOOSH	1. Zero drank it.
FEET	2. Sweet ___; Clyde's nickname
LAUGHING	3. Miss Barlow was doing this when she died.
RED	4. Color of Warden's hair and nails
ONLY	5. Lullaby: If ___; if ___.
WARDEN	6. Woman who ran the camp
THUMBS	7. Signal Stanley & Zero gave: ___ up
HOLES	8. Title of the book
PEACHES	9. Katherine made these.
BOAT	10. Zero hid under it.
HECTOR	11. Zero's real name
ZERO	12. He escaped from the camp before Stanley did.
DONKEY	13. Original Mary Lou was Sam's ___.
SPAT	14. What each boy did when he finished digging his hole
SEEDS	15. Mr. Sir ate sunflower ___.
WRECK	16. Sign on the rec room door: ____ Room
PENDANSKI	17. Name of the counselor
TEACHER	18. Katherine Barlow's original profession
GREEN	19. Camp ___ Lake
VENOM	20. Ingredient in Warden's nail polish

Holes Matching 1

___ 1. SACHAR   A. Stanley's nickname
___ 2. LIZARDS   B. What Zero could not do
___ 3. ONLY   C. These were in the suitcase Stanley & Zero found.
___ 4. TEACHER   D. Miss Barlow was doing this when she died.
___ 5. THUMBS   E. Stanley found a ___ tube in the hole he dug.
___ 6. SPAT   F. Zero hid under it.
___ 7. BASEBALL   G. Camp ___ Lake
___ 8. LIPSTICK   H. Title of the book
___ 9. JEWELS   I. Sweet ___; Clyde's nickname
___10. BOAT   J. What each boy did when he finished digging his hole
___11. LAUGHING   K. He referred to a Girl Scout camp: Mr. ___
___12. FEET   L. Zero drank it.
___13. CAVEMAN   M. He escaped from the camp before Stanley did.
___14. BARLOW   N. Sam's boat: Mary ___
___15. ZERO   O. Stanley's great-great-grandfather
___16. VENOM   P. Color of Warden's hair and nails
___17. SIR   Q. Sam offered these as a remedy.
___18. READ   R. Lullaby: If ___; if ___.
___19. RED   S. Ingredient in Warden's nail polish
___20. HOLES   T. Katherine Barlow's original profession
___21. SPLOOSH   U. Dangerous, yellow-spotted ones inhabited the area.
___22. LOU   V. Author
___23. GREEN   W. Signal Stanley & Zero gave: ___ up
___24. ONIONS   X. Game Clyde Livingston played
___25. ELYA   Y. Katherine's last name

Holes Matching 1 Answer Key

V - 1.	SACHAR	A.	Stanley's nickname
U - 2.	LIZARDS	B.	What Zero could not do
R - 3.	ONLY	C.	These were in the suitcase Stanley & Zero found.
T - 4.	TEACHER	D.	Miss Barlow was doing this when she died.
W - 5.	THUMBS	E.	Stanley found a ___ tube in the hole he dug.
J - 6.	SPAT	F.	Zero hid under it.
X - 7.	BASEBALL	G.	Camp ___ Lake
E - 8.	LIPSTICK	H.	Title of the book
C - 9.	JEWELS	I.	Sweet ___; Clyde's nickname
F - 10.	BOAT	J.	What each boy did when he finished digging his hole
D - 11.	LAUGHING	K.	He referred to a Girl Scout camp: Mr. ___
I - 12.	FEET	L.	Zero drank it.
A - 13.	CAVEMAN	M.	He escaped from the camp before Stanley did.
Y - 14.	BARLOW	N.	Sam's boat: Mary ___
M - 15.	ZERO	O.	Stanley's great-great-grandfather
S - 16.	VENOM	P.	Color of Warden's hair and nails
K - 17.	SIR	Q.	Sam offered these as a remedy.
B - 18.	READ	R.	Lullaby: If ___; if ___.
P - 19.	RED	S.	Ingredient in Warden's nail polish
H - 20.	HOLES	T.	Katherine Barlow's original profession
L - 21.	SPLOOSH	U.	Dangerous, yellow-spotted ones inhabited the area.
N - 22.	LOU	V.	Author
G - 23.	GREEN	W.	Signal Stanley & Zero gave: ___ up
Q - 24.	ONIONS	X.	Game Clyde Livingston played
O - 25.	ELYA	Y.	Katherine's last name

Holes Matching 2

___ 1. GYPSY   A. Stanley's last name
___ 2. LIZARDS   B. Stanley's great-great-grandfather
___ 3. CAVEMAN   C. Game Clyde Livingston played
___ 4. YELNATS   D. Digging utensil
___ 5. ONIONS   E. Stanley's nickname
___ 6. ZERO   F. Sam offered these as a remedy.
___ 7. ONLY   G. He escaped from the camp before Stanley did.
___ 8. ZIGZAG   H. Sweet ___; Clyde's nickname
___ 9. PEACHES   I. Katherine made these.
___10. SACHAR   J. A one-legged one put a curse on the family
___11. RED   K. Original Mary Lou was Sam's ___.
___12. BASEBALL   L. Katherine's last name
___13. DONKEY   M. Sam's boat: Mary ___
___14. WARDEN   N. Madame who was a one-legged Gypsy
___15. ELYA   O. Color of Warden's hair and nails
___16. ZERONI   P. Zero attacked him when he started to beat Stanley.
___17. SIR   Q. Stanley found a ___ tube in the hole he dug.
___18. HECTOR   R. He referred to a Girl Scout camp: Mr. ___
___19. HOLES   S. Author
___20. FEET   T. Miss Barlow was doing this when she died.
___21. LIPSTICK   U. Lullaby: If ___; if ___.
___22. SHOVEL   V. Dangerous, yellow-spotted ones inhabited the area.
___23. LOU   W. Title of the book
___24. BARLOW   X. Woman who ran the camp
___25. LAUGHING   Y. Zero's real name

Holes Matching 2 Answer Key

J - 1. GYPSY		A. Stanley's last name
V - 2. LIZARDS		B. Stanley's great-great-grandfather
E - 3. CAVEMAN		C. Game Clyde Livingston played
A - 4. YELNATS		D. Digging utensil
F - 5. ONIONS		E. Stanley's nickname
G - 6. ZERO		F. Sam offered these as a remedy.
U - 7. ONLY		G. He escaped from the camp before Stanley did.
P - 8. ZIGZAG		H. Sweet ___; Clyde's nickname
I - 9. PEACHES		I. Katherine made these.
S -10. SACHAR		J. A one-legged one put a curse on the family
O -11. RED		K. Original Mary Lou was Sam's ___.
C -12. BASEBALL		L. Katherine's last name
K -13. DONKEY		M. Sam's boat: Mary ___
X -14. WARDEN		N. Madame who was a one-legged Gypsy
B -15. ELYA		O. Color of Warden's hair and nails
N -16. ZERONI		P. Zero attacked him when he started to beat Stanley.
R -17. SIR		Q. Stanley found a ___ tube in the hole he dug.
Y -18. HECTOR		R. He referred to a Girl Scout camp: Mr. ___
W -19. HOLES		S. Author
H -20. FEET		T. Miss Barlow was doing this when she died.
Q -21. LIPSTICK		U. Lullaby: If ___; if ___.
D -22. SHOVEL		V. Dangerous, yellow-spotted ones inhabited the area.
M -23. LOU		W. Title of the book
L -24. BARLOW		X. Woman who ran the camp
T -25. LAUGHING		Y. Zero's real name

Holes Matching 3

___ 1. BASEBALL	A. Dangerous, yellow-spotted ones inhabited the area.
___ 2. MOM	B. A one-legged one put a curse on the family
___ 3. SPAT	C. These were in the suitcase Stanley & Zero found.
___ 4. ZERONI	D. Name of the counselor
___ 5. VENOM	E. Lullaby: If ___; if ___.
___ 6. READ	F. Title of the book
___ 7. ONIONS	G. Author
___ 8. SEEDS	H. Katherine's last name
___ 9. PEACHES	I. Mr. Sir ate sunflower ___.
___10. SACHAR	J. Mr. Pendanski's nickname
___11. LIPSTICK	K. He escaped from the camp before Stanley did.
___12. FEET	L. Madame who was a one-legged Gypsy
___13. ELYA	M. Zero attacked him when he started to beat Stanley.
___14. ZIGZAG	N. Stanley found a ___ tube in the hole he dug.
___15. WARDEN	O. Sweet ___; Clyde's nickname
___16. ZERO	P. Stanley's great-great-grandfather
___17. GYPSY	Q. Game Clyde Livingston played
___18. LIZARDS	R. What each boy did when he finished digging his hole
___19. DONKEY	S. Signal Stanley & Zero gave: ___ up
___20. ONLY	T. Original Mary Lou was Sam's ___.
___21. PENDANSKI	U. What Zero could not do
___22. THUMBS	V. Ingredient in Warden's nail polish
___23. BARLOW	W. Sam offered these as a remedy.
___24. JEWELS	X. Woman who ran the camp
___25. HOLES	Y. Katherine made these.

Holes Matching 3 Answer Key

Q - 1. BASEBALL	A.	Dangerous, yellow-spotted ones inhabited the area.
J - 2. MOM	B.	A one-legged one put a curse on the family
R - 3. SPAT	C.	These were in the suitcase Stanley & Zero found.
L - 4. ZERONI	D.	Name of the counselor
V - 5. VENOM	E.	Lullaby: If ___; if ___.
U - 6. READ	F.	Title of the book
W - 7. ONIONS	G.	Author
I - 8. SEEDS	H.	Katherine's last name
Y - 9. PEACHES	I.	Mr. Sir ate sunflower ___.
G -10. SACHAR	J.	Mr. Pendanski's nickname
N -11. LIPSTICK	K.	He escaped from the camp before Stanley did.
O -12. FEET	L.	Madame who was a one-legged Gypsy
P -13. ELYA	M.	Zero attacked him when he started to beat Stanley.
M -14. ZIGZAG	N.	Stanley found a ___ tube in the hole he dug.
X -15. WARDEN	O.	Sweet ___; Clyde's nickname
K -16. ZERO	P.	Stanley's great-great-grandfather
B -17. GYPSY	Q.	Game Clyde Livingston played
A -18. LIZARDS	R.	What each boy did when he finished digging his hole
T -19. DONKEY	S.	Signal Stanley & Zero gave: ___ up
E -20. ONLY	T.	Original Mary Lou was Sam's ___.
D -21. PENDANSKI	U.	What Zero could not do
S -22. THUMBS	V.	Ingredient in Warden's nail polish
H -23. BARLOW	W.	Sam offered these as a remedy.
C -24. JEWELS	X.	Woman who ran the camp
F -25. HOLES	Y.	Katherine made these.

Holes Matching 4

___ 1. JEWELS   A. Zero's real name
___ 2. WATER   B. Madame who was a one-legged Gypsy
___ 3. YELNATS   C. Sam offered these as a remedy.
___ 4. HECTOR   D. Stanley's last name
___ 5. BOAT   E. Woman who ran the camp
___ 6. THUMBS   F. Sam's boat: Mary ___
___ 7. ONIONS   G. Name of the counselor
___ 8. BARLOW   H. Zero drank it.
___ 9. GYPSY   I. Katherine made these.
___10. CAVEMAN   J. Signal Stanley & Zero gave: ___ up
___11. FEET   K. Title of the book
___12. LOU   L. These were in the suitcase Stanley & Zero found.
___13. DONKEY   M. What Zero could not do
___14. PEACHES   N. Stanley found a ___ tube in the hole he dug.
___15. WARDEN   O. Sweet ___; Clyde's nickname
___16. TEACHER   P. Kind of truck Stanley stole and wrecked
___17. ZERO   Q. Katherine Barlow's original profession
___18. READ   R. A one-legged one put a curse on the family
___19. SHOVEL   S. Original Mary Lou was Sam's ___.
___20. SPLOOSH   T. Katherine's last name
___21. GREEN   U. Digging utensil
___22. HOLES   V. Stanley's nickname
___23. ZERONI   W. Camp ___ Lake
___24. LIPSTICK   X. Zero hid under it.
___25. PENDANSKI   Y. He escaped from the camp before Stanley did.

Holes Matching 4 Answer Key

L - 1. JEWELS		A. Zero's real name
P - 2. WATER		B. Madame who was a one-legged Gypsy
D - 3. YELNATS		C. Sam offered these as a remedy.
A - 4. HECTOR		D. Stanley's last name
X - 5. BOAT		E. Woman who ran the camp
J - 6. THUMBS		F. Sam's boat: Mary ___
C - 7. ONIONS		G. Name of the counselor
T - 8. BARLOW		H. Zero drank it.
R - 9. GYPSY		I. Katherine made these.
V - 10. CAVEMAN		J. Signal Stanley & Zero gave: ___ up
O - 11. FEET		K. Title of the book
F - 12. LOU		L. These were in the suitcase Stanley & Zero found.
S - 13. DONKEY		M. What Zero could not do
I - 14. PEACHES		N. Stanley found a ___ tube in the hole he dug.
E - 15. WARDEN		O. Sweet ___; Clyde's nickname
Q - 16. TEACHER		P. Kind of truck Stanley stole and wrecked
Y - 17. ZERO		Q. Katherine Barlow's original profession
M - 18. READ		R. A one-legged one put a curse on the family
U - 19. SHOVEL		S. Original Mary Lou was Sam's ___.
H - 20. SPLOOSH		T. Katherine's last name
W - 21. GREEN		U. Digging utensil
K - 22. HOLES		V. Stanley's nickname
B - 23. ZERONI		W. Camp ___ Lake
N - 24. LIPSTICK		X. Zero hid under it.
G - 25. PENDANSKI		Y. He escaped from the camp before Stanley did.

Copyrighted

Holes Magic Squares 1

Match the definition with the vocabulary word. Put your answers in the magic squares below. When your answers are correct, all columns and rows will add to the same number.

A. DONKEY
B. SHOVEL
C. LOU
D. CAVEMAN
E. WARDEN
F. SEEDS
G. THUMBS
H. BASEBALL
I. YELNATS
J. WATER
K. GYPSY
L. ZIGZAG
M. ONIONS
N. RED
O. ZERONI
P. BOAT

1. Game Clyde Livingston played
2. Sam offered these as a remedy.
3. Digging utensil
4. A one-legged one put a curse on the family
5. Kind of truck Stanley stole and wrecked
6. Sam's boat: Mary ___
7. Zero hid under it.
8. Woman who ran the camp
9. Madame who was a one-legged Gypsy
10. Mr. Sir ate sunflower ___.
11. Stanley's last name
12. Stanley's nickname
13. Original Mary Lou was Sam's ___.
14. Zero attacked him when he started to beat Stanley.
15. Signal Stanley & Zero gave: ___ up
16. Color of Warden's hair and nails

A=	B=	C=	D=
E=	F=	G=	H=
I=	J=	K=	L=
M=	N=	O=	P=

Holes Magic Squares 1 Answer Key

Match the definition with the vocabulary word. Put your answers in the magic squares below. When your answers are correct, all columns and rows will add to the same number.

A. DONKEY	E. WARDEN	I. YELNATS	M. ONIONS
B. SHOVEL	F. SEEDS	J. WATER	N. RED
C. LOU	G. THUMBS	K. GYPSY	O. ZERONI
D. CAVEMAN	H. BASEBALL	L. ZIGZAG	P. BOAT

1. Game Clyde Livingston played
2. Sam offered these as a remedy.
3. Digging utensil
4. A one-legged one put a curse on the family
5. Kind of truck Stanley stole and wrecked
6. Sam's boat: Mary ___
7. Zero hid under it.
8. Woman who ran the camp
9. Madame who was a one-legged Gypsy
10. Mr. Sir ate sunflower ___.
11. Stanley's last name
12. Stanley's nickname
13. Original Mary Lou was Sam's ___.
14. Zero attacked him when he started to beat Stanley.
15. Signal Stanley & Zero gave: ___ up
16. Color of Warden's hair and nails

A=13	B=3	C=6	D=12
E=8	F=10	G=15	H=1
I=11	J=5	K=4	L=14
M=2	N=16	O=9	P=7

Holes Magic Squares 2

Match the definition with the vocabulary word. Put your answers in the magic squares below. When your answers are correct, all columns and rows will add to the same number.

A. RED
B. PEACHES
C. WRECK
D. WARDEN
E. ONLY
F. GYPSY
G. CAVEMAN
H. PENDANSKI
I. WATER
J. HOLES
K. BASEBALL
L. VENOM
M. SEEDS
N. DONKEY
O. YELNATS
P. JEWELS

1. A one-legged one put a curse on the family
2. Kind of truck Stanley stole and wrecked
3. Stanley's last name
4. Woman who ran the camp
5. Mr. Sir ate sunflower ___.
6. Katherine made these.
7. Name of the counselor
8. Game Clyde Livingston played
9. Sign on the rec room door: ____ Room
10. These were in the suitcase Stanley & Zero found.
11. Title of the book
12. Lullaby: If ___; if ___.
13. Ingredient in Warden's nail polish
14. Stanley's nickname
15. Color of Warden's hair and nails
16. Original Mary Lou was Sam's ___.

A=	B=	C=	D=
E=	F=	G=	H=
I=	J=	K=	L=
M=	N=	O=	P=

Holes Magic Squares 2 Answer Key

Match the definition with the vocabulary word. Put your answers in the magic squares below. When your answers are correct, all columns and rows will add to the same number.

A. RED
B. PEACHES
C. WRECK
D. WARDEN
E. ONLY
F. GYPSY
G. CAVEMAN
H. PENDANSKI
I. WATER
J. HOLES
K. BASEBALL
L. VENOM
M. SEEDS
N. DONKEY
O. YELNATS
P. JEWELS

1. A one-legged one put a curse on the family
2. Kind of truck Stanley stole and wrecked
3. Stanley's last name
4. Woman who ran the camp
5. Mr. Sir ate sunflower ___.
6. Katherine made these.
7. Name of the counselor
8. Game Clyde Livingston played
9. Sign on the rec room door: ____ Room
10. These were in the suitcase Stanley & Zero found.
11. Title of the book
12. Lullaby: If ___; if ___.
13. Ingredient in Warden's nail polish
14. Stanley's nickname
15. Color of Warden's hair and nails
16. Original Mary Lou was Sam's ___.

A=15	B=6	C=9	D=4
E=12	F=1	G=14	H=7
I=2	J=11	K=8	L=13
M=5	N=16	O=3	P=10

Holes Magic Squares 3

Match the definition with the vocabulary word. Put your answers in the magic squares below. When your answers are correct, all columns and rows will add to the same number.

A. WARDEN
B. SHOVEL
C. BOAT
D. VENOM
E. FEET
F. TEACHER
G. READ
H. THUMBS
I. ONLY
J. MOM
K. WATER
L. SPLOOSH
M. HOLES
N. HECTOR
O. SIR
P. SEEDS

1. Zero hid under it.
2. Mr. Pendanski's nickname
3. Katherine Barlow's original profession
4. He referred to a Girl Scout camp: Mr. ___
5. Mr. Sir ate sunflower ___.
6. Sweet ___; Clyde's nickname
7. Lullaby: If ___; if ___.
8. Ingredient in Warden's nail polish
9. Title of the book
10. Signal Stanley & Zero gave: ___ up
11. Zero drank it.
12. Woman who ran the camp
13. Digging utensil
14. Kind of truck Stanley stole and wrecked
15. What Zero could not do
16. Zero's real name

A=	B=	C=	D=
E=	F=	G=	H=
I=	J=	K=	L=
M=	N=	O=	P=

25
Copyrighted

Holes Magic Squares 3 Answer Key

Match the definition with the vocabulary word. Put your answers in the magic squares below. When your answers are correct, all columns and rows will add to the same number.

A. WARDEN
B. SHOVEL
C. BOAT
D. VENOM
E. FEET
F. TEACHER
G. READ
H. THUMBS
I. ONLY
J. MOM
K. WATER
L. SPLOOSH
M. HOLES
N. HECTOR
O. SIR
P. SEEDS

1. Zero hid under it.
2. Mr. Pendanski's nickname
3. Katherine Barlow's original profession
4. He referred to a Girl Scout camp: Mr. ___
5. Mr. Sir ate sunflower ___.
6. Sweet ___; Clyde's nickname
7. Lullaby: If ___; if ___.
8. Ingredient in Warden's nail polish
9. Title of the book
10. Signal Stanley & Zero gave: ___ up
11. Zero drank it.
12. Woman who ran the camp
13. Digging utensil
14. Kind of truck Stanley stole and wrecked
15. What Zero could not do
16. Zero's real name

A=12	B=13	C=1	D=8
E=6	F=3	G=15	H=10
I=7	J=2	K=14	L=11
M=9	N=16	O=4	P=5

Holes Magic Squares 4

Match the definition with the vocabulary word. Put your answers in the magic squares below. When your answers are correct, all columns and rows will add to the same number.

A. LAUGHING   E. ONIONS   I. SPLOOSH   M. BASEBALL
B. READ   F. ELYA   J. TEACHER   N. LIZARDS
C. SIR   G. SEEDS   K. WARDEN   O. JEWELS
D. RED   H. ONLY   L. ZERO   P. VENOM

1. Game Clyde Livingston played
2. Stanley's great-great-grandfather
3. Lullaby: If ___; if ___.
4. These were in the suitcase Stanley & Zero found.
5. He escaped from the camp before Stanley did.
6. He referred to a Girl Scout camp: Mr. ___
7. Miss Barlow was doing this when she died.
8. Katherine Barlow's original profession
9. Woman who ran the camp
10. Color of Warden's hair and nails
11. What Zero could not do
12. Zero drank it.
13. Dangerous, yellow-spotted ones inhabited the area.
14. Sam offered these as a remedy.
15. Mr. Sir ate sunflower ___.
16. Ingredient in Warden's nail polish

A=	B=	C=	D=
E=	F=	G=	H=
I=	J=	K=	L=
M=	N=	O=	P=

Holes Magic Squares 4 Answer Key

Match the definition with the vocabulary word. Put your answers in the magic squares below. When your answers are correct, all columns and rows will add to the same number.

A. LAUGHING   E. ONIONS   I. SPLOOSH   M. BASEBALL
B. READ   F. ELYA   J. TEACHER   N. LIZARDS
C. SIR   G. SEEDS   K. WARDEN   O. JEWELS
D. RED   H. ONLY   L. ZERO   P. VENOM

1. Game Clyde Livingston played
2. Stanley's great-great-grandfather
3. Lullaby: If ___; if ___.
4. These were in the suitcase Stanley & Zero found.
5. He escaped from the camp before Stanley did.
6. He referred to a Girl Scout camp: Mr. ___
7. Miss Barlow was doing this when she died.
8. Katherine Barlow's original profession
9. Woman who ran the camp
10. Color of Warden's hair and nails
11. What Zero could not do
12. Zero drank it.
13. Dangerous, yellow-spotted ones inhabited the area.
14. Sam offered these as a remedy.
15. Mr. Sir ate sunflower ___.
16. Ingredient in Warden's nail polish

A=7	B=11	C=6	D=10
E=14	F=2	G=15	H=3
I=12	J=8	K=9	L=5
M=1	N=13	O=4	P=16

Holes Word Search 1

Words are placed backwards, forward, diagonally, up and down. Clues listed below can help you find the words. Circle the hidden vocabulary words in the maze.

```
O N I O N S D F J C P V V J C Z L N Y D
J R Y T N F R O J E B L D E A I I J E V
V H C Q X K K T N K L F K W V G Z D L T
T B L N C Z P D X K P B B E E Z A X N V
L L A B E S A B Z T E M W L M A R Q A W
D Y U P P N Q H E E Z Y Z S A G D Y T G
P L G Z S H P E C A P D D B N S S P S R
N C H K T S F L C C P Q T Q Y F V G G G
R G I N F H N S V H S E T Q R H R B C B
L B N F N Q W L P E Z B A Z N W A G H F
Q R G L P W R J P R K Q C C M D H X J L
Q W H D S H C Y W V B V B M H P C V I W
Z N Q N B V L T C X M X J N P E A P P R
T T N C Q B H B C R H S O O L P S K W Y
Q Q K P Q D A H B K T G H R B T P A F Y
Z Q L Y A R G D O J S B T W I H R Z X Z
M E M E L M G W D L H L Q C V D X X F S
Z E R O N L Y W A T E R K C E R W U B D
B E W O M V P D G V C S L N N P O M T J
D J N D N H S G O M T D K D O L U C W T
G R E E N I Y H Y J O S I R M H E L Y A
B O A T W D S N L Y R S P A T S E E D S
```

A one-legged one put a curse on the family (5)
Author (6)
Camp ___ Lake (5)
Color of Warden's hair and nails (3)
Dangerous, yellow-spotted ones inhabited the area. (7)
Digging utensil (6)
Game Clyde Livingston played (8)
He escaped from the camp before Stanley did. (4)
He referred to a Girl Scout camp: Mr. ___ (3)
Ingredient in Warden's nail polish (5)
Katherine Barlow's original profession (7)
Katherine made these. (7)
Katherine's last name (6)
Kind of truck Stanley stole and wrecked (5)
Lullaby: If ___; if ___. (4)
Madame who was a one-legged Gypsy (6)
Miss Barlow was doing this when she died. (8)
Mr. Pendanski's nickname (3)
Mr. Sir ate sunflower ___. (5)
Name of the counselor (9)
Original Mary Lou was Sam's ___. (6)

Sam offered these as a remedy. (6)
Sam's boat: Mary ___ (3)
Sign on the rec room door: ____ Room (5)
Signal Stanley & Zero gave: ___ up (6)
Stanley found a ___ tube in the hole he dug. (8)
Stanley's great-great-grandfather (4)
Stanley's last name (7)
Stanley's nickname (7)
Sweet ___; Clyde's nickname (4)
These were in the suitcase Stanley & Zero found. (6)
Title of the book (5)
What Zero could not do (4)
What each boy did when he finished digging his hole (4)
Woman who ran the camp (6)
Zero attacked him when he started to beat Stanley. (6)
Zero drank it. (7)
Zero hid under it. (4)
Zero's real name (6)

Holes Word Search 1 Answer Key

Words are placed backwards, forward, diagonally, up and down. Clues listed below can help you find the words. Circle the hidden vocabulary words in the maze.

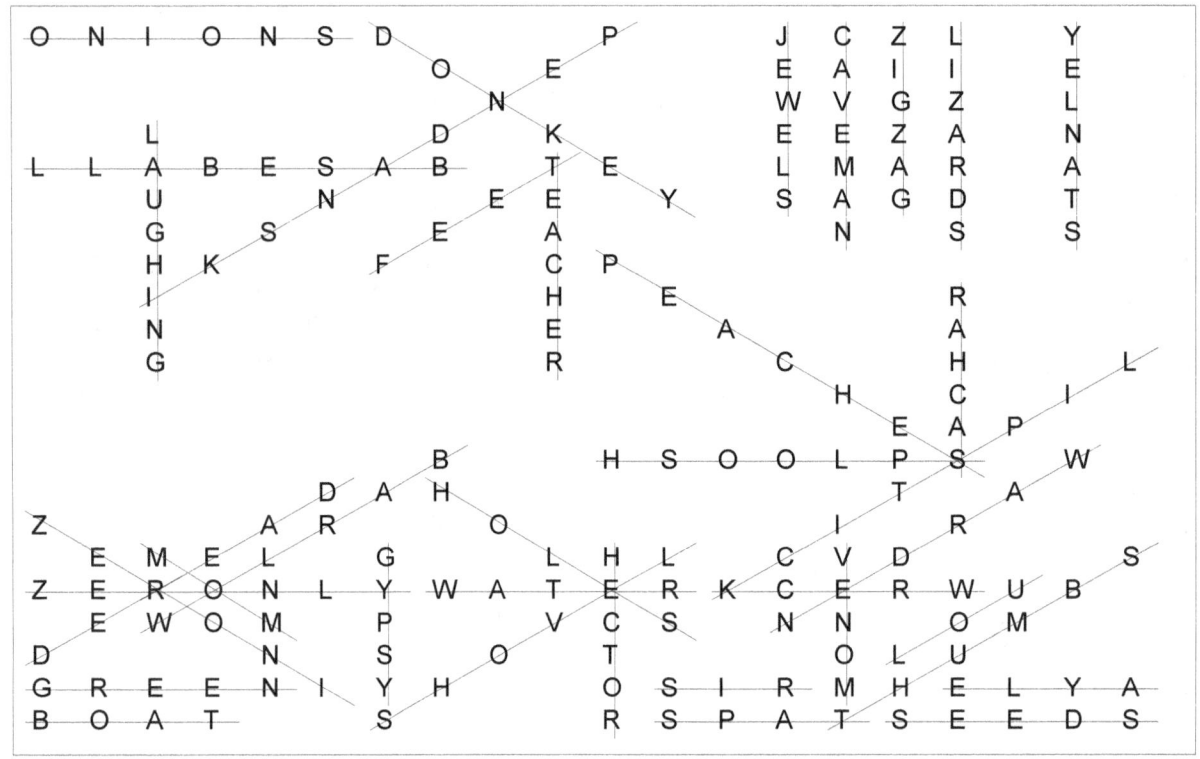

A one-legged one put a curse on the family (5)
Author (6)
Camp ___ Lake (5)
Color of Warden's hair and nails (3)
Dangerous, yellow-spotted ones inhabited the area. (7)
Digging utensil (6)
Game Clyde Livingston played (8)
He escaped from the camp before Stanley did. (4)
He referred to a Girl Scout camp: Mr. ___ (3)
Ingredient in Warden's nail polish (5)
Katherine Barlow's original profession (7)
Katherine made these. (7)
Katherine's last name (6)
Kind of truck Stanley stole and wrecked (5)
Lullaby: If ___; if ___. (4)
Madame who was a one-legged Gypsy (6)
Miss Barlow was doing this when she died. (8)
Mr. Pendanski's nickname (3)
Mr. Sir ate sunflower ___. (5)
Name of the counselor (9)
Original Mary Lou was Sam's ___. (6)

Sam offered these as a remedy. (6)
Sam's boat: Mary ___ (3)
Sign on the rec room door: ___ Room (5)
Signal Stanley & Zero gave: ___ up (6)
Stanley found a ___ tube in the hole he dug. (8)
Stanley's great-great-grandfather (4)
Stanley's last name (7)
Stanley's nickname (7)
Sweet ___; Clyde's nickname (4)
These were in the suitcase Stanley & Zero found. (6)
Title of the book (5)
What Zero could not do (4)
What each boy did when he finished digging his hole (4)
Woman who ran the camp (6)
Zero attacked him when he started to beat Stanley. (6)
Zero drank it. (7)
Zero hid under it. (4)
Zero's real name (6)

Holes Word Search 2

Words are placed backwards, forward, diagonally, up and down. Clues listed below can help you find the words. Circle the hidden vocabulary words in the maze.

```
E X Q F K L H S T A N L E Y E K N O D D
L P Q C E W E T E B N S R V B K Y B V J
Y B E V Z E C M A F G R D J A P Y A E K
A R O H S J T Q C M B O A T S E Q R N F
W H W N S L O P H Z O B V B E N D L O D
S W A P C C R K E S D M K M B D K O M K
R L T C X K S D R D A Y Z R A A L W Q C
C J E R S D G F G Q D C T T L N J L Z X
Z A R V R Z B Z R N L C H P L S N X J P
N Q V A B Q W F Q J H J T A B K B D C P
J S Z E J V V M G C Z V D Y R I Z Z Y P
L I C L M R X D P S G R T Q J F X W M G
L A D T Q A T Q G E F O L G K C S C D D
F J U M C D N T F H J W N C J B H D N N
W V B G B V L D G C Z K I I M Q O S E K
W N Z N H S N H Z A N T C U O L L S D Y
S T Q R L I S G S E S O H P B N E Y R G
P H Z E R O N I S P A T N S I R S O A M
J H W D O Z U G I H X E D L E P R Z W B
N E B L V Q D L R F E R Q A Y E G P S P
J N P P V Z G Z D R K Q D G Z I D H G J
Z S X P P T C G G K V K F H Z V R S Z M
```

A one-legged one put a curse on the family (5)
Author (6)
Camp ___ Lake (5)
Color of Warden's hair and nails (3)
Dangerous, yellow-spotted ones inhabited the area. (7)
Digging utensil (6)
Game Clyde Livingston played (8)
He escaped from the camp before Stanley did. (4)
He referred to a Girl Scout camp: Mr. ___ (3)
Ingredient in Warden's nail polish (5)
Katherine Barlow's original profession (7)
Katherine made these. (7)
Katherine's last name (6)
Kind of truck Stanley stole and wrecked (5)
Lullaby: If ___; if ___. (4)
Madame who was a one-legged Gypsy (6)
Miss Barlow was doing this when she died. (8)
Mr. Pendanski's nickname (3)
Mr. Sir ate sunflower ___. (5)
Name of the counselor (9)
Original Mary Lou was Sam's ___. (6)
Sam offered these as a remedy. (6)
Sam's boat: Mary ___ (3)
Sign on the rec room door: ____ Room (5)
Signal Stanley & Zero gave: ___ up (6)
Stanley found a ___ tube in the hole he dug. (8)
Stanley's great-great-grandfather (4)
Stanley's last name (7)
Stanley's nickname (7)
Sweet ___; Clyde's nickname (4)
These were in the suitcase Stanley & Zero found. (6)
Title of the book (5)
What Zero could not do (4)
What each boy did when he finished digging his hole (4)
Woman who ran the camp (6)
Zero attacked him when he started to beat Stanley. (6)
Zero drank it. (7)
Zero hid under it. (4)
Zero's real name (6)

Holes Word Search 2 Answer Key

Words are placed backwards, forward, diagonally, up and down. Clues listed below can help you find the words. Circle the hidden vocabulary words in the maze.

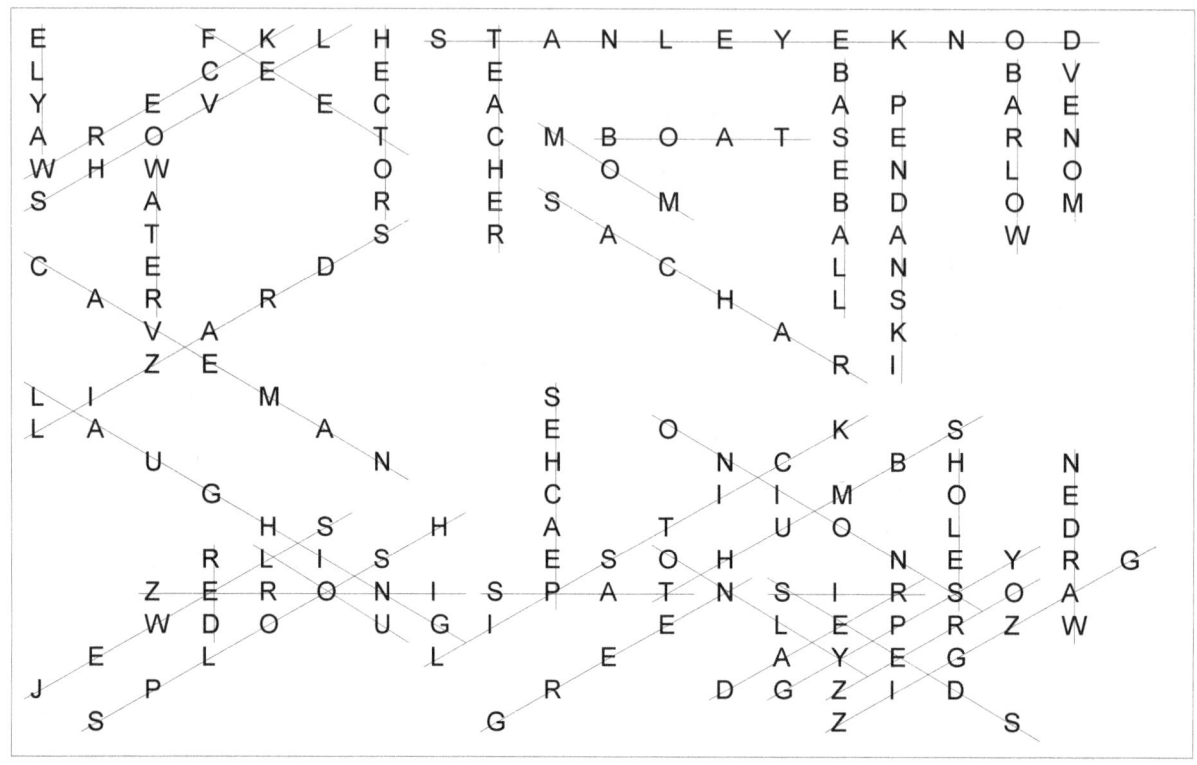

A one-legged one put a curse on the family (5)
Author (6)
Camp ___ Lake (5)
Color of Warden's hair and nails (3)
Dangerous, yellow-spotted ones inhabited the area. (7)
Digging utensil (6)
Game Clyde Livingston played (8)
He escaped from the camp before Stanley did. (4)
He referred to a Girl Scout camp: Mr. ___ (3)
Ingredient in Warden's nail polish (5)
Katherine Barlow's original profession (7)
Katherine made these. (7)
Katherine's last name (6)
Kind of truck Stanley stole and wrecked (5)
Lullaby: If ___; if ___. (4)
Madame who was a one-legged Gypsy (6)
Miss Barlow was doing this when she died. (8)
Mr. Pendanski's nickname (3)
Mr. Sir ate sunflower ___. (5)
Name of the counselor (9)
Original Mary Lou was Sam's ___. (6)

Sam offered these as a remedy. (6)
Sam's boat: Mary ___ (3)
Sign on the rec room door: ____ Room (5)
Signal Stanley & Zero gave: ___ up (6)
Stanley found a ___ tube in the hole he dug. (8)
Stanley's great-great-grandfather (4)
Stanley's last name (7)
Stanley's nickname (7)
Sweet ___; Clyde's nickname (4)
These were in the suitcase Stanley & Zero found. (6)
Title of the book (5)
What Zero could not do (4)
What each boy did when he finished digging his hole (4)
Woman who ran the camp (6)
Zero attacked him when he started to beat Stanley. (6)
Zero drank it. (7)
Zero hid under it. (4)
Zero's real name (6)

Holes Word Search 3

Words are placed backwards, forward, diagonally, up and down. Words listed below are included in the maze. Circle the hidden vocabulary words in the maze.

```
R T S G V Q D D S M D S E H C A E P L G
E V A Y D E A R O L T H E K M H V L T S
D X C P Q E N L C N C O L E S F A Q H V
L Z H S R L Y O I L K V T O D B L M U Z
L I A Y B A K F M Z F E O D E S I C M N
W G R M Y A K M C M A L Y S F H P H B V
M Z Q L L F R D M M P R A F G K S V S C
P A E T P X G L K S O B D N W T T X S Z
F G R E E N C H O D N G X S B T I C H K
V T M T N F R R L W I L S C R M C Q P Z
B L D L D D R X L R O C S G S X K B W Z
Z B G N A C V Z N I N M Q W D W C Q X B
C V R L N D F P N R S M J X Y V Q Y B L
K B B V S X C O N X X Y L Q L L C R N G
Y H Z T K B R A F K Z P A P R C Z W X W
Z E K F I E L Y V S P Y U Q D L A L H F
H T L X Z B V C S E V M G Q S R C S K V
Y D V N M O Z P H L M S H Z D L F L W C
R Z F B A A A E V O D A I E Q O S E R V
D Q W W A T E R R H Y L N O C U I W E X
Q H V F Q J S X Z O R M G D C C R E C T
H E C T O R E H C A E T M O M M N J K S
```

BARLOW	GYPSY	MOM	SEEDS	WARDEN
BASEBALL	HECTOR	ONIONS	SHOVEL	WATER
BOAT	HOLES	ONLY	SIR	WRECK
CAVEMAN	JEWELS	PEACHES	SPAT	YELNATS
DONKEY	LAUGHING	PENDANSKI	SPLOOSH	ZERO
ELYA	LIPSTICK	READ	TEACHER	ZERONI
FEET	LIZARDS	RED	THUMBS	ZIGZAG
GREEN	LOU	SACHAR	VENOM	

Holes Word Search 3 Answer Key

Words are placed backwards, forward, diagonally, up and down. Words listed below are included in the maze. Circle the hidden vocabulary words in the maze.

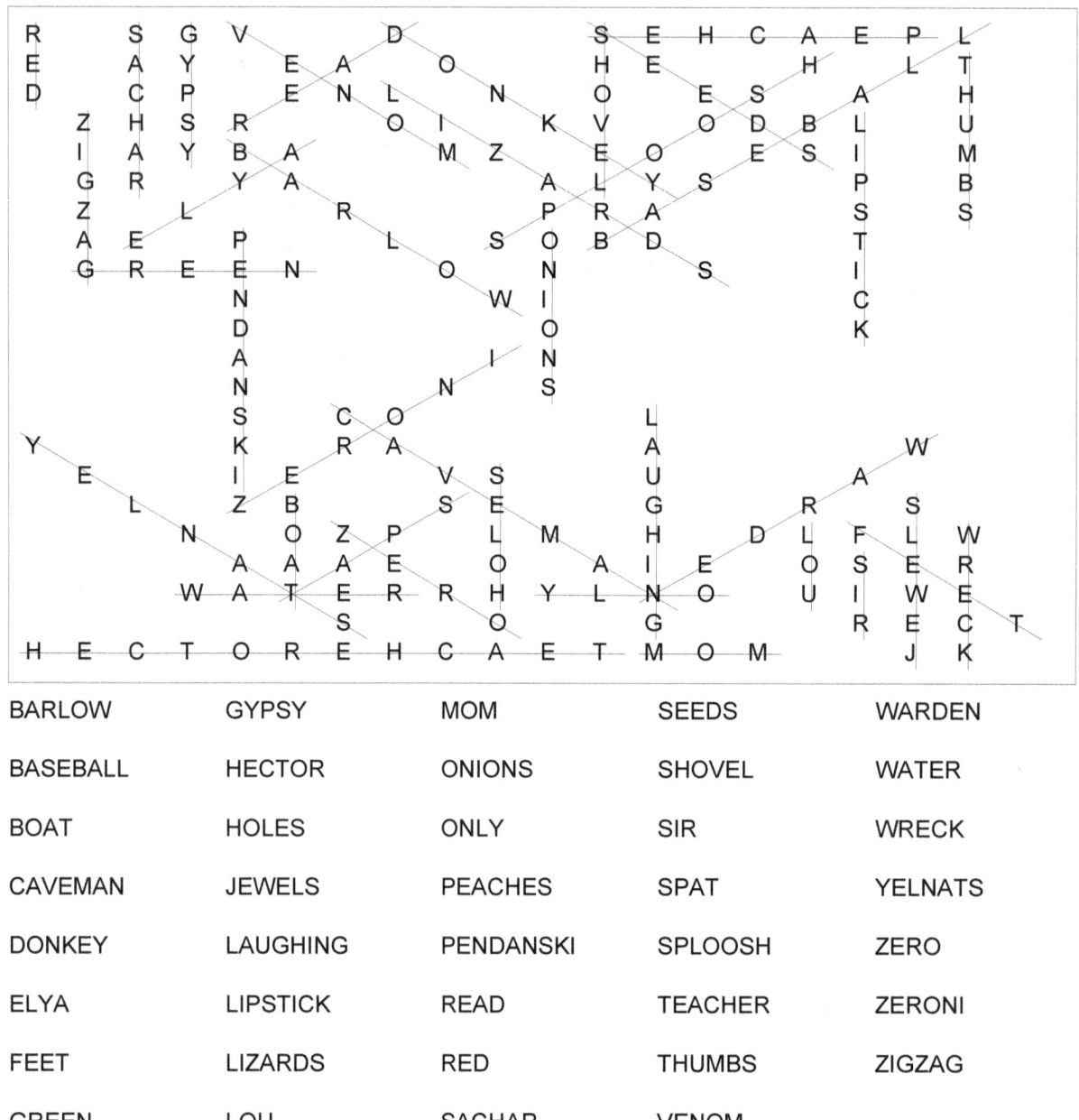

BARLOW	GYPSY	MOM	SEEDS	WARDEN
BASEBALL	HECTOR	ONIONS	SHOVEL	WATER
BOAT	HOLES	ONLY	SIR	WRECK
CAVEMAN	JEWELS	PEACHES	SPAT	YELNATS
DONKEY	LAUGHING	PENDANSKI	SPLOOSH	ZERO
ELYA	LIPSTICK	READ	TEACHER	ZERONI
FEET	LIZARDS	RED	THUMBS	ZIGZAG
GREEN	LOU	SACHAR	VENOM	

Holes Word Search 4

Words are placed backwards, forward, diagonally, up and down. Words listed below are included in the maze. Circle the hidden vocabulary words in the maze.

```
W S A C H A R S C F W O L R A B F N L B
R W Z Y J G D G J F F C N W Q P G F I G
E K S Y M E X R W P P M Z L A X S S Z N
C X R B E S T L J D B L W S Y T B J A T
K J V S C A V E M A N V E N O M E P R P
R D Y P Z M J X A P Y S D F U W S R D C
D Z K D B N G T D C G J R H E R G T S Y
L I P S T I C K B H H G T L D O N K E Y
T X B N P L Q K F Z Y E S L P T C X Y V
P P B S C I C W J P Z G R A D C W Y L W
Z R T L J K F T J R K Q D B S E B J L M
R Y Y C V S H S X H B D S E Q H F F V W
F B G L C N R J J M T T R S Z P L Q G L
L G J K N A L N H B P D N A M Z B C T R
F T Y W J D C W S F W Y P B B G W H V H
Q S T P F N Z B P B B S Q F N S S L F R
C E S R E E S F L Z S P G I O B P N E R
D H I D Z P M H O N I Y H R R D O A E X
B C R H H Z E R O N I G L Y E L N A T S
D A Q R G V X I S V U M Z R Z F D Y T P
W E M Z Q T N G H A E V O A P K H L L D
G P S E L O H X L U O L D M G R E E N J
```

BARLOW	GYPSY	MOM	SEEDS	WARDEN
BASEBALL	HECTOR	ONIONS	SHOVEL	WATER
BOAT	HOLES	ONLY	SIR	WRECK
CAVEMAN	JEWELS	PEACHES	SPAT	YELNATS
DONKEY	LAUGHING	PENDANSKI	SPLOOSH	ZERO
ELYA	LIPSTICK	READ	TEACHER	ZERONI
FEET	LIZARDS	RED	THUMBS	ZIGZAG
GREEN	LOU	SACHAR	VENOM	

Holes Word Search 4 Answer Key

Words are placed backwards, forward, diagonally, up and down. Words listed below are included in the maze. Circle the hidden vocabulary words in the maze.

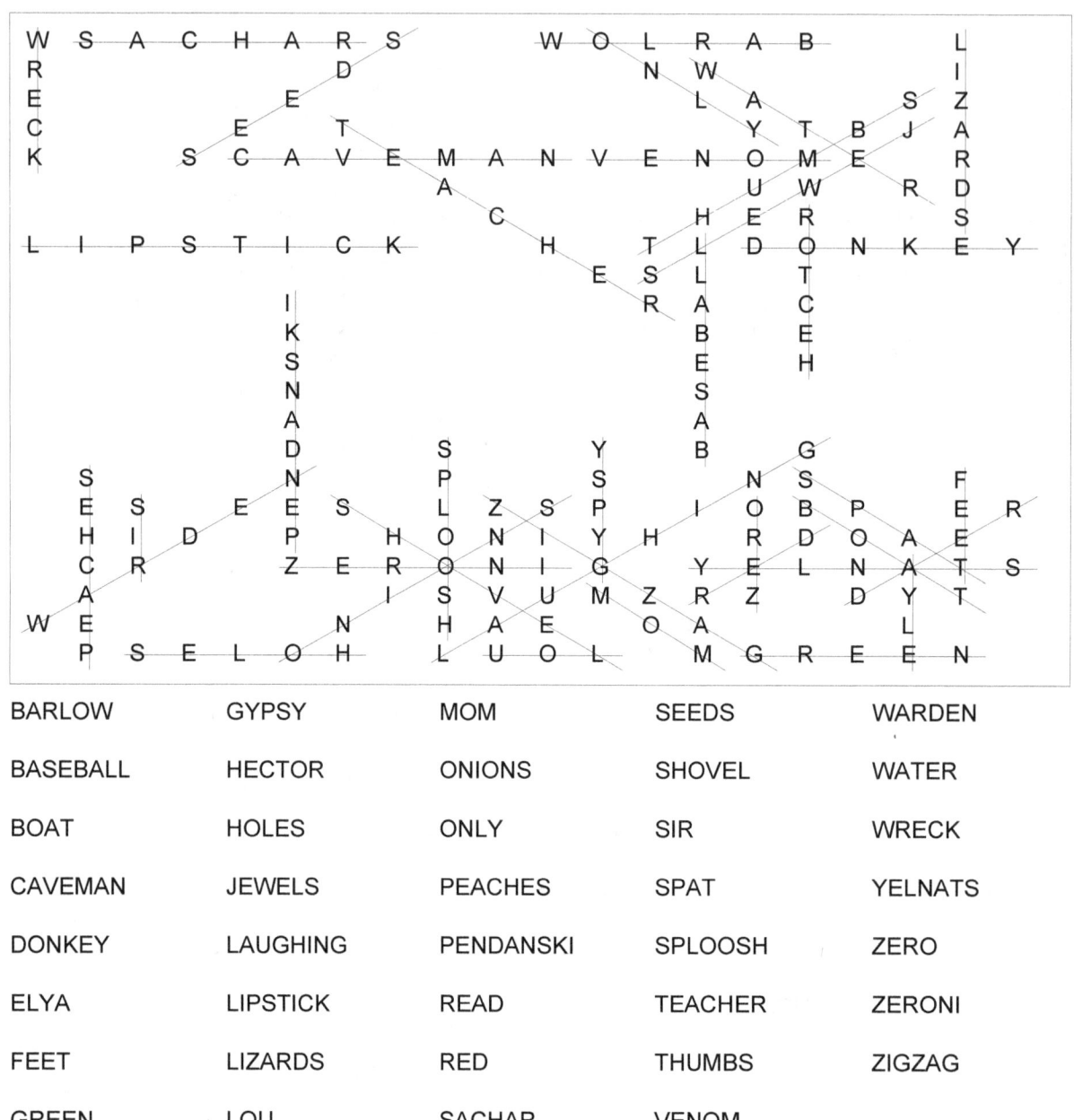

BARLOW	GYPSY	MOM	SEEDS	WARDEN
BASEBALL	HECTOR	ONIONS	SHOVEL	WATER
BOAT	HOLES	ONLY	SIR	WRECK
CAVEMAN	JEWELS	PEACHES	SPAT	YELNATS
DONKEY	LAUGHING	PENDANSKI	SPLOOSH	ZERO
ELYA	LIPSTICK	READ	TEACHER	ZERONI
FEET	LIZARDS	RED	THUMBS	ZIGZAG
GREEN	LOU	SACHAR	VENOM	

Holes Crossword 1

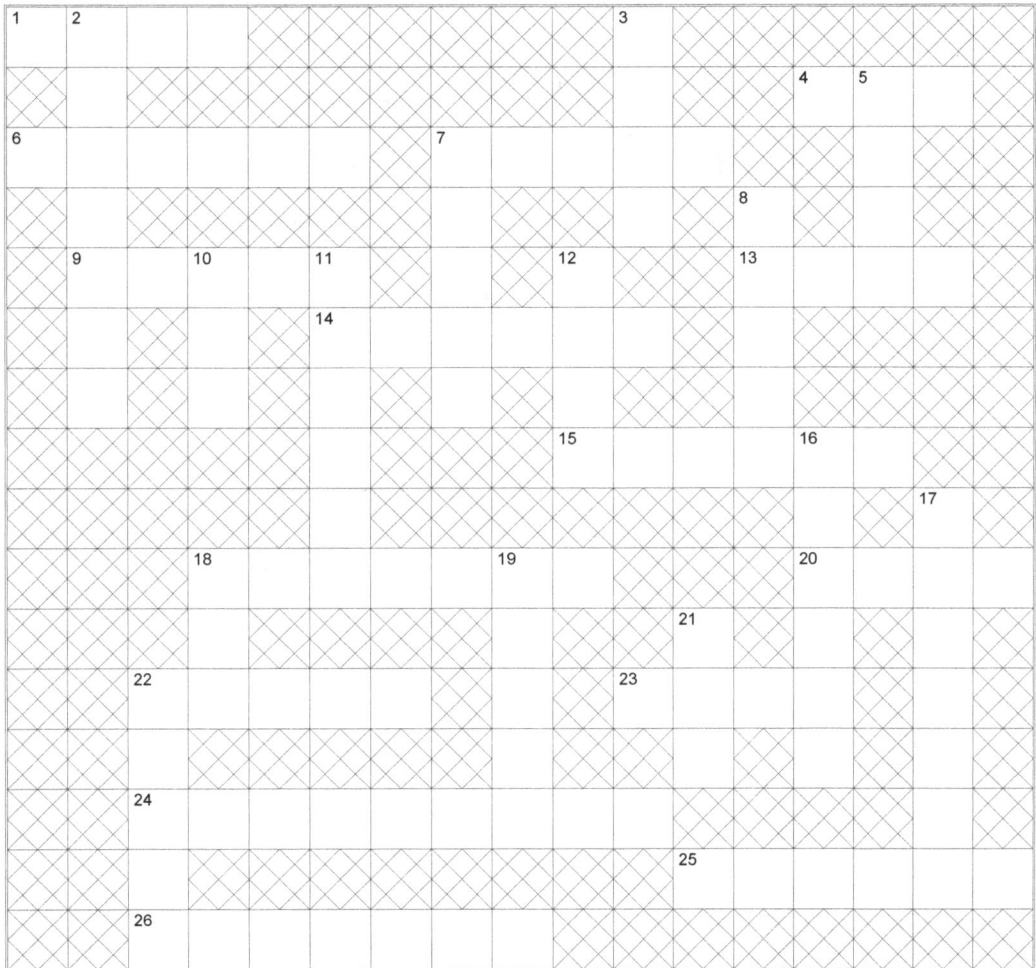

Across
1. What each boy did when he finished digging his hole
4. Mr. Pendanski's nickname
6. Woman who ran the camp
7. Kind of truck Stanley stole and wrecked
9. Title of the book
13. Stanley's great-great-grandfather
14. Zero's real name
15. Signal Stanley & Zero gave: ___ up
18. Zero drank it.
20. What Zero could not do
22. Camp ___ Lake
23. He escaped from the camp before Stanley did.
24. Name of the counselor
25. Sam offered these as a remedy.
26. Stanley's last name

Down
2. Katherine made these.
3. Sweet ___; Clyde's nickname
5. Lullaby: If ___; if ___.
7. Sign on the rec room door: ____ Room
8. Ingredient in Warden's nail polish
10. Sam's boat: Mary ___
11. Digging utensil
12. Zero hid under it.
16. Katherine's last name
17. Stanley's nickname
18. He referred to a Girl Scout camp: Mr. ___
19. Mr. Sir ate sunflower ___.
21. Color of Warden's hair and nails
22. A one-legged one put a curse on the family

Holes Crossword 1 Answer Key

	1 S	2 P	A	T					3 F				
		E							E		4 M	5 O	M
6 W	A	R	D	E	N		7 W	A	T	E	R		N
	C						R		T		8 V		L
	9 H		10 O	11 S			E		12 B		13 E	L	Y	A
	E		O		14 H	E	C	T	O	R		N		
	S		U		O		K		A			O		
			V					15 T	H	U	M	16 B	S	
			E									A		17 C
			18 S	P	L	O	O	19 S	H		20 R	E	A	D
			I					E		21 R		L		V
		22 G	R	E	E	N		E		23 Z	E	R	O	E
		Y						D		D		W		M
	24 P	E	N	D	A	N	S	K	I					A
	S								25 O	N	I	O	N	S
	26 Y	E	L	N	A	T	S							

Across
1. What each boy did when he finished digging his hole
4. Mr. Pendanski's nickname
6. Woman who ran the camp
7. Kind of truck Stanley stole and wrecked
9. Title of the book
13. Stanley's great-great-grandfather
14. Zero's real name
15. Signal Stanley & Zero gave: ___ up
18. Zero drank it.
20. What Zero could not do
22. Camp ___ Lake
23. He escaped from the camp before Stanley did.
24. Name of the counselor
25. Sam offered these as a remedy.
26. Stanley's last name

Down
2. Katherine made these.
3. Sweet ___; Clyde's nickname
5. Lullaby: If ___; if ___.
7. Sign on the rec room door: ____ Room
8. Ingredient in Warden's nail polish
10. Sam's boat: Mary ___
11. Digging utensil
12. Zero hid under it.
16. Katherine's last name
17. Stanley's nickname
18. He referred to a Girl Scout camp: Mr. ___
19. Mr. Sir ate sunflower ___.
21. Color of Warden's hair and nails
22. A one-legged one put a curse on the family

Holes Crossword 2

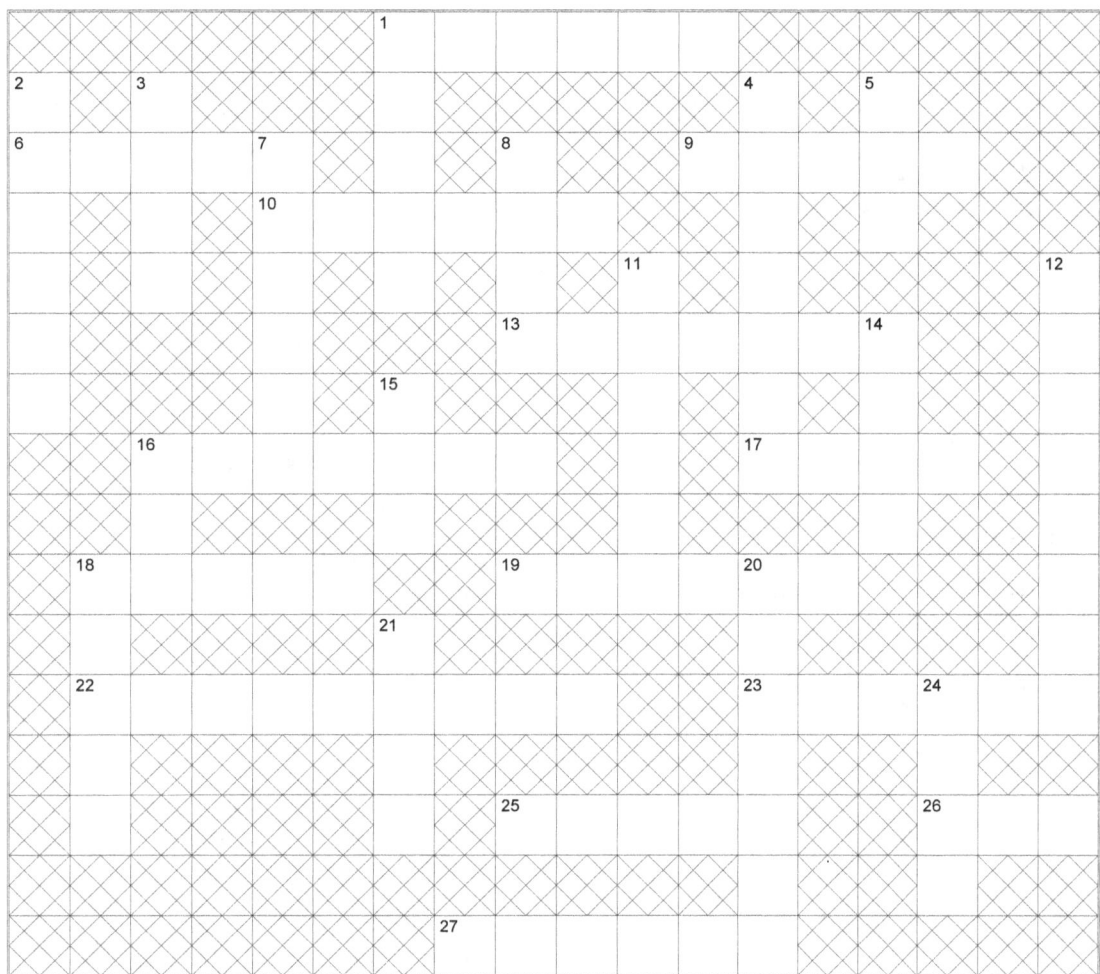

Across
1. Woman who ran the camp
6. Title of the book
9. Ingredient in Warden's nail polish
10. Zero's real name
13. Katherine Barlow's original profession
16. Zero drank it.
17. What each boy did when he finished digging his hole
18. Camp ___ Lake
19. These were in the suitcase Stanley & Zero found.
22. Name of the counselor
23. Zero attacked him when he started to beat Stanley.
25. Kind of truck Stanley stole and wrecked
26. Color of Warden's hair and nails
27. Sam offered these as a remedy.

Down
1. Sign on the rec room door: ____ Room
2. Signal Stanley & Zero gave: ___ up
3. Stanley's great-great-grandfather
4. Katherine made these.
5. Mr. Pendanski's nickname
7. Digging utensil
8. Zero hid under it.
11. Katherine's last name
12. Miss Barlow was doing this when she died.
14. What Zero could not do
15. Sam's boat: Mary ___
16. He referred to a Girl Scout camp: Mr. ___
18. A one-legged one put a curse on the family
20. Dangerous, yellow-spotted ones inhabited the area.
21. Lullaby: If ___; if ___.
24. He escaped from the camp before Stanley did.

Holes Crossword 2 Answer Key

```
            1
            W  A  R  D  E  N
 2     3                     4   5
 T     E        R            P   M
 6     7        8      9
 H  O  L  E  S  E     B     V  E  N  O  M
           10
 U     Y        H  E  C  T  O  R     A  M
                                11            12
 M     A        O     K     A   B     C      L
                                13         14
 B     V                    T  E  A  C  H  E  R     A
                      15
 S     E              L           R     E     U
           16                           17
           S  P  L  O  O  S  H     L    S  P  A  T  G
           I              U        O       D     H
           18                    19       20
           G  R  E  E  N          J  E  W  E  L  S     I
           Y              21                  I         N
           22                                23       24
           P  E  N  D  A  N  S  K  I         Z  I  G  Z  A  G
           S                 L                A        E
                                      25                 26
           Y                 Y         W  A  T  E  R     R  E  D
                                                  D     O
                                    27
                                    O  N  I  O  N  S
```

Across
1. Woman who ran the camp
6. Title of the book
9. Ingredient in Warden's nail polish
10. Zero's real name
13. Katherine Barlow's original profession
16. Zero drank it.
17. What each boy did when he finished digging his hole
18. Camp ___ Lake
19. These were in the suitcase Stanley & Zero found.
22. Name of the counselor
23. Zero attacked him when he started to beat Stanley.
25. Kind of truck Stanley stole and wrecked
26. Color of Warden's hair and nails
27. Sam offered these as a remedy.

Down
1. Sign on the rec room door: ____ Room
2. Signal Stanley & Zero gave: ___ up
3. Stanley's great-great-grandfather
4. Katherine made these.
5. Mr. Pendanski's nickname
7. Digging utensil
8. Zero hid under it.
11. Katherine's last name
12. Miss Barlow was doing this when she died.
14. What Zero could not do
15. Sam's boat: Mary ___
16. He referred to a Girl Scout camp: Mr. ___
18. A one-legged one put a curse on the family
20. Dangerous, yellow-spotted ones inhabited the area.
21. Lullaby: If ___; if ___.
24. He escaped from the camp before Stanley did.

Holes Crossword 3

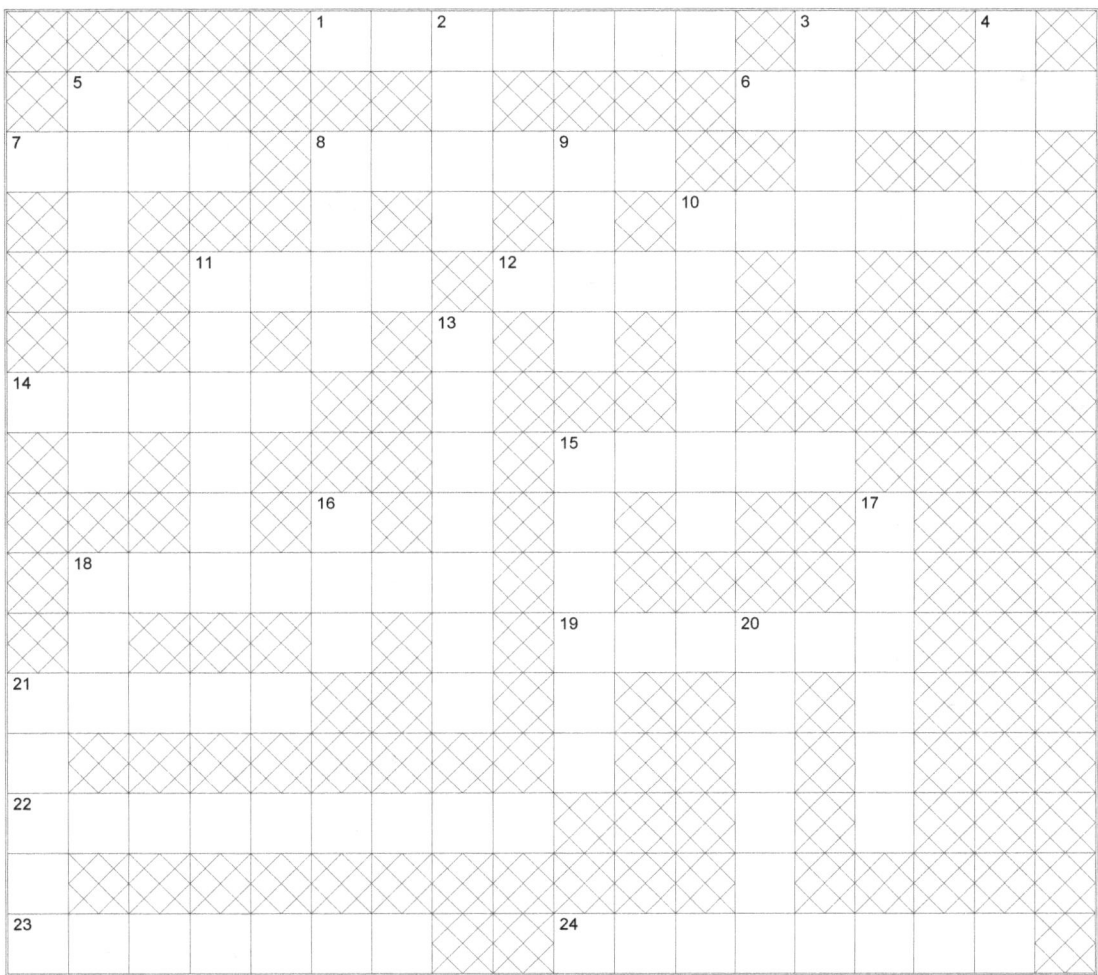

Across
1. Dangerous, yellow-spotted ones inhabited the area.
6. Original Mary Lou was Sam's ___.
7. What Zero could not do
8. Katherine's last name
10. Sign on the rec room door: ____ Room
11. What each boy did when he finished digging his hole
12. Stanley's great-great-grandfather
14. Ingredient in Warden's nail polish
15. Mr. Sir ate sunflower ___.
18. Zero drank it.
19. Zero's real name
21. Camp ___ Lake
22. Name of the counselor
23. Stanley's last name
24. Stanley found a ___ tube in the hole he dug.

Down
2. He escaped from the camp before Stanley did.
3. Title of the book
4. Color of Warden's hair and nails
5. Katherine made these.
8. Zero hid under it.
9. Lullaby: If ___; if ___.
10. Woman who ran the camp
11. Digging utensil
13. Katherine Barlow's original profession
15. Author
16. Mr. Pendanski's nickname
17. Madame who was a one-legged Gypsy
18. He referred to a Girl Scout camp: Mr. ___
20. Signal Stanley & Zero gave: ___ up
21. A one-legged one put a curse on the family

Holes Crossword 3 Answer Key

					¹L	²I	Z	A	R	D	S		³H			⁴R
	⁵P					Z						⁶D	O	N	K	E	Y
⁷R	E	A	D		⁸B	A	R	L	O	W			L			D
	A				O		O		N		¹⁰W	R	E	C	K	
	C	¹¹S	P	A	T		¹²E	L	Y	A		S				
	H	H			T		¹³T		Y		R					
¹⁴V	E	N	O	M			E				D					
	S	V					A		¹⁵S	E	E	D	S			
		E		¹⁶M		C		A		N			¹⁷Z		
	¹⁸S	P	L	O	O	S	H		C				E		
		I			M			¹⁹H	E	C	²⁰T	O	R		
²¹G	R	E	E	N			R		A		H		O		
Y									R		U		N		
²²P	E	N	D	A	N	S	K	I		M		I		
S									B				
²³Y	E	L	N	A	T	S		²⁴L	I	P	S	T	I	C	K

Across
1. Dangerous, yellow-spotted ones inhabited the area.
6. Original Mary Lou was Sam's ___.
7. What Zero could not do
8. Katherine's last name
10. Sign on the rec room door: ____ Room
11. What each boy did when he finished digging his hole
12. Stanley's great-great-grandfather
14. Ingredient in Warden's nail polish
15. Mr. Sir ate sunflower ___.
18. Zero drank it.
19. Zero's real name
21. Camp ___ Lake
22. Name of the counselor
23. Stanley's last name
24. Stanley found a ___ tube in the hole he dug.

Down
2. He escaped from the camp before Stanley did.
3. Title of the book
4. Color of Warden's hair and nails
5. Katherine made these.
8. Zero hid under it.
9. Lullaby: If ___; if ___.
10. Woman who ran the camp
11. Digging utensil
13. Katherine Barlow's original profession
15. Author
16. Mr. Pendanski's nickname
17. Madame who was a one-legged Gypsy
18. He referred to a Girl Scout camp: Mr. ___
20. Signal Stanley & Zero gave: ___ up
21. A one-legged one put a curse on the family

Holes Crossword 4

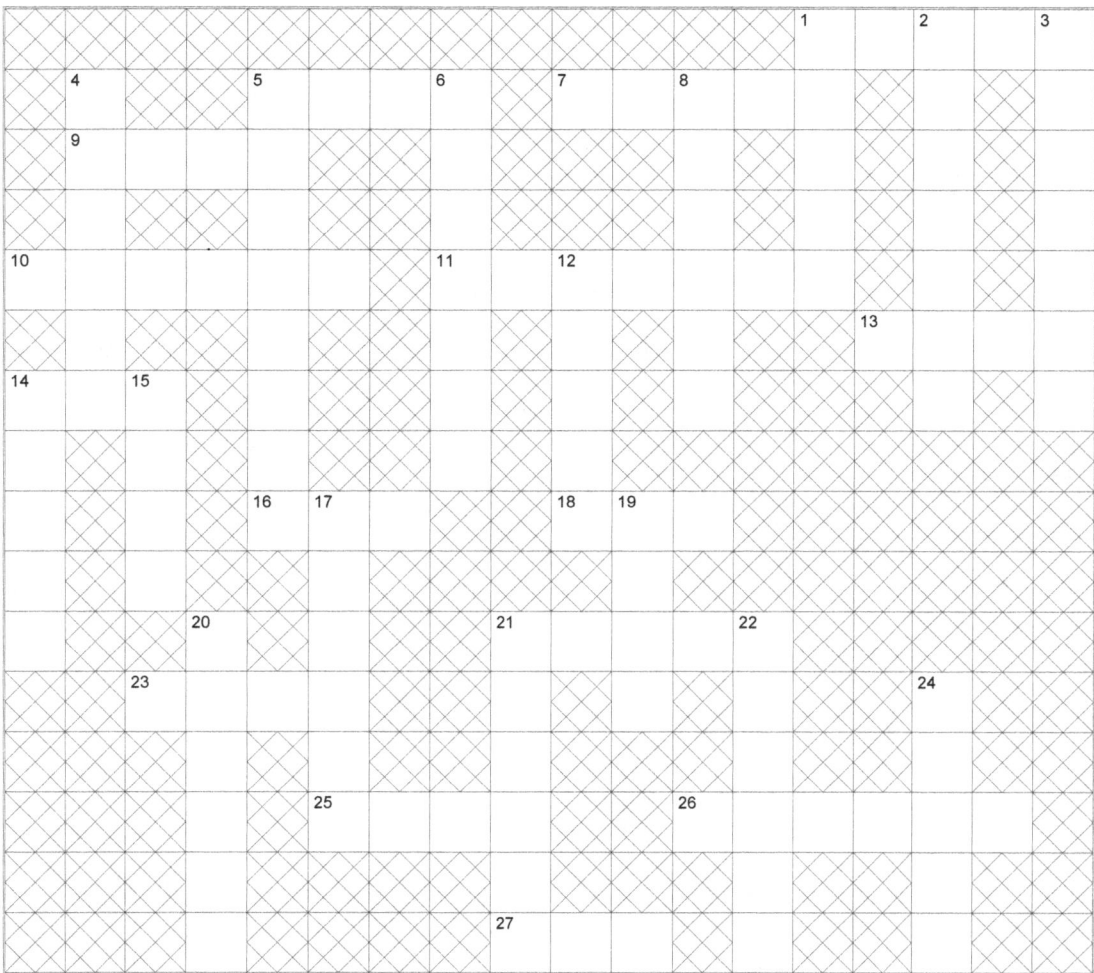

Across
1. A one-legged one put a curse on the family
5. Zero hid under it.
7. Kind of truck Stanley stole and wrecked
9. Stanley's great-great-grandfather
10. Original Mary Lou was Sam's ___.
11. Stanley's nickname
13. Sweet ___; Clyde's nickname
14. He referred to a Girl Scout camp: Mr. ___
16. Sam's boat: Mary ___
18. Mr. Pendanski's nickname
21. Title of the book
23. He escaped from the camp before Stanley did.
25. What each boy did when he finished digging his hole
26. Digging utensil
27. Color of Warden's hair and nails

Down
1. Camp ___ Lake
2. Katherine made these.
3. Stanley's last name
4. Madame who was a one-legged Gypsy
5. Game Clyde Livingston played
6. Katherine Barlow's original profession
8. Signal Stanley & Zero gave: ___ up
12. Ingredient in Warden's nail polish
14. Mr. Sir ate sunflower ___.
15. What Zero could not do
17. Sam offered these as a remedy.
19. Lullaby: If ___; if ___.
20. These were in the suitcase Stanley & Zero found.
21. Zero's real name
22. Author
24. Sign on the rec room door: ____ Room

Holes Crossword 4 Answer Key

										1 G	2 P	3 Y
	4 Z		5 B	O	A	6 T		7 W	A	T	E	R		8 E			Y			P			S			Y		E
9 E	L	Y	A		E		H		E	A	L
R		S		A		U		E		C		N
10 D	O	N	K	E	Y		11 C	A	12 V	E	M	A	N		13 F	E	E	T
	N		B		H		E		B						S		S
14 S	15 I	R	A		E		N		S			
E	E		L		R		O				
	16 A	17 L	O	U		18 M	19 O	M			
E	D	D		N			N				
S		20 J		I		21 H	O	L	E	22 S		
		23 Z	E	R	O		E		Y		A		24 W
		W		N			C				C		R
		E	25 S	P	A	T		26 S	H	O	V	E	L
		L				O			A			C
		S		27 R	E	D		R			K

Across
1. A one-legged one put a curse on the family
5. Zero hid under it.
7. Kind of truck Stanley stole and wrecked
9. Stanley's great-great-grandfather
10. Original Mary Lou was Sam's ___.
11. Stanley's nickname
13. Sweet ___; Clyde's nickname
14. He referred to a Girl Scout camp: Mr. ___
16. Sam's boat: Mary ___
18. Mr. Pendanski's nickname
21. Title of the book
23. He escaped from the camp before Stanley did.
25. What each boy did when he finished digging his hole
26. Digging utensil
27. Color of Warden's hair and nails

Down
1. Camp ___ Lake
2. Katherine made these.
3. Stanley's last name
4. Madame who was a one-legged Gypsy
5. Game Clyde Livingston played
6. Katherine Barlow's original profession
8. Signal Stanley & Zero gave: ___ up
12. Ingredient in Warden's nail polish
14. Mr. Sir ate sunflower ___.
15. What Zero could not do
17. Sam offered these as a remedy.
19. Lullaby: If ___; if ___.
20. These were in the suitcase Stanley & Zero found.
21. Zero's real name
22. Author
24. Sign on the rec room door: ____ Room

Holes

ZIGZAG	DONKEY	LOU	PEACHES	BOAT
PENDANSKI	BARLOW	SEEDS	THUMBS	GYPSY
SHOVEL	HECTOR	FREE SPACE	SPAT	SPLOOSH
HOLES	LIZARDS	FEET	ZERO	ZERONI
CAVEMAN	WATER	LAUGHING	READ	SACHAR

Holes

JEWELS	GREEN	VENOM	BASEBALL	SIR
ONLY	MOM	ELYA	TEACHER	YELNATS
RED	WARDEN	FREE SPACE	LIPSTICK	SACHAR
READ	LAUGHING	WATER	CAVEMAN	ZERONI
ZERO	FEET	LIZARDS	HOLES	SPLOOSH

Holes

READ	CAVEMAN	FEET	DONKEY	THUMBS
LAUGHING	SACHAR	ELYA	RED	PENDANSKI
VENOM	SPAT	FREE SPACE	LIZARDS	SPLOOSH
SEEDS	WATER	HOLES	HECTOR	BASEBALL
WARDEN	MOM	LIPSTICK	ONLY	GREEN

Holes

JEWELS	GYPSY	PEACHES	ONIONS	SIR
BARLOW	ZERO	SHOVEL	BOAT	TEACHER
ZIGZAG	LOU	FREE SPACE	YELNATS	GREEN
ONLY	LIPSTICK	MOM	WARDEN	BASEBALL
HECTOR	HOLES	WATER	SEEDS	SPLOOSH

Holes

GYPSY	BOAT	READ	GREEN	HECTOR
ONLY	LIZARDS	PEACHES	LAUGHING	WARDEN
JEWELS	HOLES	FREE SPACE	SEEDS	BARLOW
SIR	ONIONS	TEACHER	FEET	DONKEY
WATER	WRECK	ZIGZAG	SPAT	MOM

Holes

THUMBS	LIPSTICK	SHOVEL	LOU	SPLOOSH
VENOM	SACHAR	ZERONI	PENDANSKI	CAVEMAN
ZERO	BASEBALL	FREE SPACE	ELYA	MOM
SPAT	ZIGZAG	WRECK	WATER	DONKEY
FEET	TEACHER	ONIONS	SIR	BARLOW

Holes

WATER	YELNATS	SPAT	SIR	GREEN
ELYA	SPLOOSH	THUMBS	RED	SACHAR
LAUGHING	SHOVEL	FREE SPACE	PENDANSKI	CAVEMAN
ONLY	LIZARDS	WRECK	BARLOW	MOM
VENOM	LIPSTICK	BOAT	GYPSY	JEWELS

Holes

ZERONI	FEET	HECTOR	PEACHES	TEACHER
LOU	READ	DONKEY	ONIONS	ZERO
WARDEN	HOLES	FREE SPACE	BASEBALL	JEWELS
GYPSY	BOAT	LIPSTICK	VENOM	MOM
BARLOW	WRECK	LIZARDS	ONLY	CAVEMAN

Holes

SEEDS	SACHAR	FEET	HOLES	BARLOW
SPLOOSH	LOU	BASEBALL	MOM	DONKEY
SPAT	TEACHER	FREE SPACE	JEWELS	CAVEMAN
ONLY	LIPSTICK	SIR	SHOVEL	PEACHES
ZERO	LAUGHING	RED	WARDEN	YELNATS

Holes

THUMBS	GYPSY	LIZARDS	PENDANSKI	WRECK
VENOM	READ	ZERONI	BOAT	ZIGZAG
WATER	HECTOR	FREE SPACE	ONIONS	YELNATS
WARDEN	RED	LAUGHING	ZERO	PEACHES
SHOVEL	SIR	LIPSTICK	ONLY	CAVEMAN

Holes

ZIGZAG	JEWELS	WATER	BASEBALL	GYPSY
BARLOW	YELNATS	ZERONI	CAVEMAN	LAUGHING
ONLY	MOM	FREE SPACE	LIPSTICK	THUMBS
DONKEY	ZERO	LIZARDS	ELYA	READ
SPAT	RED	PENDANSKI	SIR	SPLOOSH

Holes

ONIONS	GREEN	WRECK	FEET	PEACHES
SEEDS	HOLES	SHOVEL	SACHAR	HECTOR
WARDEN	BOAT	FREE SPACE	TEACHER	SPLOOSH
SIR	PENDANSKI	RED	SPAT	READ
ELYA	LIZARDS	ZERO	DONKEY	THUMBS

Holes

BARLOW	SPLOOSH	HECTOR	ELYA	TEACHER
READ	JEWELS	LAUGHING	SACHAR	ONLY
ZERONI	MOM	FREE SPACE	SEEDS	SIR
GREEN	LIPSTICK	DONKEY	YELNATS	LIZARDS
BOAT	ZERO	WRECK	PENDANSKI	RED

Holes

FEET	ZIGZAG	GYPSY	BASEBALL	PEACHES
SPAT	HOLES	THUMBS	SHOVEL	LOU
CAVEMAN	WATER	FREE SPACE	WARDEN	RED
PENDANSKI	WRECK	ZERO	BOAT	LIZARDS
YELNATS	DONKEY	LIPSTICK	GREEN	SIR

Holes

SIR	ONLY	VENOM	HOLES	WATER
GYPSY	WARDEN	ELYA	READ	WRECK
HECTOR	JEWELS	FREE SPACE	ZERONI	PEACHES
SHOVEL	GREEN	FEET	BOAT	SACHAR
SPAT	YELNATS	LIZARDS	RED	ZERO

Holes

BARLOW	MOM	CAVEMAN	DONKEY	TEACHER
LIPSTICK	ZIGZAG	PENDANSKI	SEEDS	LAUGHING
SPLOOSH	THUMBS	FREE SPACE	ONIONS	ZERO
RED	LIZARDS	YELNATS	SPAT	SACHAR
BOAT	FEET	GREEN	SHOVEL	PEACHES

Holes

HOLES	GREEN	MOM	PEACHES	LIZARDS
ZERONI	ELYA	SPAT	ZERO	SHOVEL
YELNATS	LOU	FREE SPACE	ONLY	BOAT
DONKEY	PENDANSKI	BARLOW	JEWELS	SACHAR
READ	WATER	GYPSY	THUMBS	ONIONS

Holes

VENOM	FEET	ZIGZAG	RED	SIR
SPLOOSH	CAVEMAN	WRECK	HECTOR	SEEDS
WARDEN	LAUGHING	FREE SPACE	BASEBALL	ONIONS
THUMBS	GYPSY	WATER	READ	SACHAR
JEWELS	BARLOW	PENDANSKI	DONKEY	BOAT

Holes

GREEN	PEACHES	READ	BASEBALL	SIR
HOLES	TEACHER	THUMBS	VENOM	SEEDS
DONKEY	SHOVEL	FREE SPACE	WRECK	ZERONI
MOM	ONLY	YELNATS	GYPSY	LIPSTICK
BARLOW	ELYA	ONIONS	PENDANSKI	LOU

Holes

ZERO	SACHAR	HECTOR	FEET	WATER
CAVEMAN	SPAT	SPLOOSH	LIZARDS	BOAT
LAUGHING	JEWELS	FREE SPACE	RED	LOU
PENDANSKI	ONIONS	ELYA	BARLOW	LIPSTICK
GYPSY	YELNATS	ONLY	MOM	ZERONI

Holes

CAVEMAN	ONIONS	SIR	ZERONI	TEACHER
HOLES	ONLY	ZIGZAG	HECTOR	GYPSY
WRECK	BARLOW	FREE SPACE	ELYA	THUMBS
SACHAR	BOAT	DONKEY	ZERO	READ
SHOVEL	LAUGHING	SPLOOSH	LIZARDS	YELNATS

Holes

MOM	FEET	SEEDS	LIPSTICK	GREEN
WATER	SPAT	PENDANSKI	VENOM	PEACHES
RED	JEWELS	FREE SPACE	BASEBALL	YELNATS
LIZARDS	SPLOOSH	LAUGHING	SHOVEL	READ
ZERO	DONKEY	BOAT	SACHAR	THUMBS

Holes

LIPSTICK	SPAT	ONIONS	LIZARDS	WRECK
VENOM	DONKEY	READ	LOU	ZIGZAG
SPLOOSH	WARDEN	FREE SPACE	TEACHER	PEACHES
GYPSY	THUMBS	CAVEMAN	ELYA	ONLY
SHOVEL	BASEBALL	BARLOW	SACHAR	WATER

Holes

YELNATS	PENDANSKI	MOM	FEET	HECTOR
GREEN	RED	BOAT	ZERONI	JEWELS
LAUGHING	HOLES	FREE SPACE	SIR	WATER
SACHAR	BARLOW	BASEBALL	SHOVEL	ONLY
ELYA	CAVEMAN	THUMBS	GYPSY	PEACHES

Holes

DONKEY	ONIONS	GYPSY	WARDEN	ONLY
CAVEMAN	WATER	BASEBALL	SACHAR	PENDANSKI
RED	WRECK	FREE SPACE	BOAT	LAUGHING
LIZARDS	GREEN	LIPSTICK	MOM	ZERONI
PEACHES	SIR	ZIGZAG	ELYA	TEACHER

Holes

LOU	HECTOR	BARLOW	SPAT	SEEDS
JEWELS	ZERO	YELNATS	SHOVEL	FEET
READ	THUMBS	FREE SPACE	SPLOOSH	TEACHER
ELYA	ZIGZAG	SIR	PEACHES	ZERONI
MOM	LIPSTICK	GREEN	LIZARDS	LAUGHING

Holes

GYPSY	ZIGZAG	SACHAR	BOAT	THUMBS
READ	ONIONS	LIPSTICK	ONLY	WRECK
HOLES	WARDEN	FREE SPACE	SPAT	YELNATS
LAUGHING	SPLOOSH	PENDANSKI	LIZARDS	ZERONI
BARLOW	FEET	SEEDS	SIR	TEACHER

Holes

GREEN	HECTOR	RED	JEWELS	CAVEMAN
BASEBALL	WATER	LOU	ZERO	DONKEY
ELYA	MOM	FREE SPACE	VENOM	TEACHER
SIR	SEEDS	FEET	BARLOW	ZERONI
LIZARDS	PENDANSKI	SPLOOSH	LAUGHING	YELNATS

Holes

BASEBALL	BARLOW	SPAT	PEACHES	THUMBS
WATER	WRECK	SPLOOSH	VENOM	ZERO
SACHAR	PENDANSKI	FREE SPACE	LOU	MOM
LIZARDS	TEACHER	WARDEN	RED	ONIONS
YELNATS	SIR	HOLES	ZIGZAG	ELYA

Holes

BOAT	ZERONI	LAUGHING	LIPSTICK	GYPSY
ONLY	READ	SEEDS	HECTOR	SHOVEL
JEWELS	DONKEY	FREE SPACE	CAVEMAN	ELYA
ZIGZAG	HOLES	SIR	YELNATS	ONIONS
RED	WARDEN	TEACHER	LIZARDS	MOM

Holes

ONIONS	WATER	ZERONI	BOAT	HECTOR
GYPSY	SPAT	LAUGHING	DONKEY	READ
WRECK	SHOVEL	FREE SPACE	HOLES	ZIGZAG
SEEDS	LIPSTICK	LOU	FEET	SPLOOSH
BARLOW	WARDEN	CAVEMAN	ONLY	MOM

Holes

VENOM	SIR	YELNATS	TEACHER	PEACHES
SACHAR	PENDANSKI	GREEN	LIZARDS	ZERO
ELYA	RED	FREE SPACE	BASEBALL	MOM
ONLY	CAVEMAN	WARDEN	BARLOW	SPLOOSH
FEET	LOU	LIPSTICK	SEEDS	ZIGZAG

Holes Vocabulary Word List

No.	Word	Clue/Definition
1.	ADJACENT	Close together; next to
2.	AMAZED	Filled with surprise; astonished
3.	APPRECIATE	Value
4.	AWKWARD	Clumsy; unskillful
5.	BARREN	Sterile; dull; unfruitful
6.	CALLUSED	Having a thickening and hardness of skin
7.	CAUTIOUS	Careful
8.	CERTAIN	Sure
9.	COMPREHEND	Understand
10.	CONCOCTIONS	Preparations made by mixing ingredients
11.	CONDEMNED	Found guilty
12.	CURSES	Appeals for evil or injury to befall someone or something
13.	DEFECTIVE	Flawed; doesn't work right
14.	DELAYED	Put off until another time
15.	DELIRIOUS	Mentally confused
16.	DESCENDANTS	Individuals from which others come; opposite of ancestors
17.	DESOLATE	Dreary; unfit for habitation or use
18.	DESPICABLE	Vile; awful
19.	DOOMED	Condemned to a severe penalty
20.	DRAWL	Speech characterized by lengthened, drawn-out vowels
21.	DREAD	Anticipate with fear, alarm, or reluctance
22.	ENGRAVED	Carved, cut, or etched into something
23.	EVAPORATED	Changed to vapor
24.	EXHAUSTED	Very tired; weary
25.	FABULOUS	Barely believable; astonishing; amazing
26.	FAMILIAR	Often encountered; known
27.	FEEBLE	Lacking strength
28.	FIERY	Very hot; like fire
29.	FLINCH	Draw away from something surprising or painful
30.	FOSSIL	Skeleton or imprint of an organism in a rock
31.	FUGITIVE	Person running away from the law
32.	GROTESQUE	Outlandish; bizarre
33.	GULLY	Deep ditch cut in the earth by running water
34.	HAZE	Moisture, dust, or vapor suspended in the air
35.	HITCHING	Hooking to; connecting
36.	HOVER	Floating or suspended in air
37.	HUMILIATING	Embarrassing; being disgraced
38.	IMAGE	Reproduction of the form of something or someone
39.	IMPROVE	Get better
40.	INCARCERATED	Shut in; confined--usually in jail
41.	INEXPLICABLE	Not able to be explained or interpreted
42.	INGREDIENT	Something that is an element; a part of
43.	INSISTS	Refuses to yield
44.	INVESTIGATION	Systematic examination
45.	JURISDICTION	Area of authority or control
46.	LEGITIMATE	Lawful; legal
47.	LOGICAL	Consistent in reasoning
48.	LOOT	Stolen goods
49.	LOPSIDED	Heavier or larger on one side than the other
50.	METALLIC	Like or containing a metal
51.	MIRAGE	An illusion; something deceptive

Holes Vocabulary Word List

No.	Word	Clue/Definition
52.	MYSTERIOUS	Not fully understood
53.	NECTAR	Delicious, invigorating drink
54.	PARCHED	Very dry
55.	PERSEVERANCE	Not giving up
56.	PIG	Jargon formed by putting first consonant at the end of a word and adding a syllable: ____ Latin
57.	PRECARIOUS	Dangerously lacking in security or stability
58.	PRECIPICE	Extremely steep or overhanging mass of rock
59.	PREPOSTEROUS	Absurd; ridiculous
60.	PROTECTED	Keep safe; guarded
61.	PROTRUDING	Sticking out; jutting out
62.	RATIO	Relation between two things
63.	REFUGE	Place of protection or shelter
64.	REQUIREMENTS	Necessary things
65.	RETRIEVED	Got back; regained
66.	SCARCITY	Shortage
67.	SCORPION	Spider-like animal with a venomous tail
68.	SHRANK	Got smaller
69.	SOGGY	Soaked with moisture
70.	SPEWED	Forced out
71.	SPRAWLED	Spread out in straggling or disorderly fashion
72.	STATIONERY	Writing paper and envelopes
73.	STIFLING	Smothering; suffocating
74.	SUBTLE	So slight as to be difficult to distinguish
75.	SUNDIAL	Instrument that indicates local solar time
76.	SUSPECT	Have doubts about; distrust
77.	SWISH	Move with a whistle or hiss
78.	TEDIOUS	Tiresome; wearisome
79.	THROBBING	Beating rapidly or violently; pounding
80.	TORMENT	Great pain or anguish
81.	URGE	Force moving one to do something
82.	VENOM	Poisonous secretion of an animal, such as a spider or snake
83.	VENTILATION	Admitting fresh air to replace stale air
84.	VISIBLE	Able to be seen
85.	WASTELAND	Uncultivated or desolate country
86.	WHEELBARROW	Vehicle with handles & a wheel used to convey loads by hand
87.	WRITHED	Twisted; squirmed

Holes Vocabulary Fill In The Blanks 1

_____ 1. Deep ditch cut in the earth by running water

_____ 2. Mentally confused

_____ 3. Soaked with moisture

_____ 4. Barely believable; astonishing; amazing

_____ 5. Person running away from the law

_____ 6. Force moving one to do something

_____ 7. Value

_____ 8. Absurd; ridiculous

_____ 9. Shut in; confined--usually in jail

_____ 10. Embarrassing; being disgraced

_____ 11. Preparations made by mixing ingredients

_____ 12. Condemned to a severe penalty

_____ 13. Keep safe; guarded

_____ 14. Vehicle with handles & a wheel used to convey loads by hand

_____ 15. Jargon formed by putting first consonant at the end of a word and adding a syllable: ___ Latin

_____ 16. Having a thickening and hardness of skin

_____ 17. Consistent in reasoning

_____ 18. Spread out in straggling or disorderly fashion

_____ 19. Clumsy; unskillful

_____ 20. Uncultivated or desolate country

Holes Vocabulary Fill In The Blanks 1 Answer Key

GULLY	1.	Deep ditch cut in the earth by running water
DELIRIOUS	2.	Mentally confused
SOGGY	3.	Soaked with moisture
FABULOUS	4.	Barely believable; astonishing; amazing
FUGITIVE	5.	Person running away from the law
URGE	6.	Force moving one to do something
APPRECIATE	7.	Value
PREPOSTEROUS	8.	Absurd; ridiculous
INCARCERATED	9.	Shut in; confined--usually in jail
HUMILIATING	10.	Embarrassing; being disgraced
CONCOCTIONS	11.	Preparations made by mixing ingredients
DOOMED	12.	Condemned to a severe penalty
PROTECTED	13.	Keep safe; guarded
WHEELBARROW	14.	Vehicle with handles & a wheel used to convey loads by hand
PIG	15.	Jargon formed by putting first consonant at the end of a word and adding a syllable: ___ Latin
CALLUSED	16.	Having a thickening and hardness of skin
LOGICAL	17.	Consistent in reasoning
SPRAWLED	18.	Spread out in straggling or disorderly fashion
AWKWARD	19.	Clumsy; unskillful
WASTELAND	20.	Uncultivated or desolate country

Holes Vocabulary Fill In The Blanks 2

_____ 1. Condemned to a severe penalty

_____ 2. Vehicle with handles & a wheel used to convey loads by hand

_____ 3. Get better

_____ 4. Dreary; unfit for habitation or use

_____ 5. Close together; next to

_____ 6. Embarrassing; being disgraced

_____ 7. Found guilty

_____ 8. Understand

_____ 9. Spider-like animal with a venomous tail

_____ 10. Force moving one to do something

_____ 11. Deep ditch cut in the earth by running water

_____ 12. Filled with surprise; astonished

_____ 13. Relation between two things

_____ 14. Area of authority or control

_____ 15. Lawful; legal

_____ 16. Spread out in straggling or disorderly fashion

_____ 17. An illusion; something deceptive

_____ 18. Careful

_____ 19. Refuses to yield

_____ 20. Keep safe; guarded

Holes Vocabulary Fill In The Blanks 2 Answer Key

DOOMED	1. Condemned to a severe penalty
WHEELBARROW	2. Vehicle with handles & a wheel used to convey loads by hand
IMPROVE	3. Get better
DESOLATE	4. Dreary; unfit for habitation or use
ADJACENT	5. Close together; next to
HUMILIATING	6. Embarrassing; being disgraced
CONDEMNED	7. Found guilty
COMPREHEND	8. Understand
SCORPION	9. Spider-like animal with a venomous tail
URGE	10. Force moving one to do something
GULLY	11. Deep ditch cut in the earth by running water
AMAZED	12. Filled with surprise; astonished
RATIO	13. Relation between two things
JURISDICTION	14. Area of authority or control
LEGITIMATE	15. Lawful; legal
SPRAWLED	16. Spread out in straggling or disorderly fashion
MIRAGE	17. An illusion; something deceptive
CAUTIOUS	18. Careful
INSISTS	19. Refuses to yield
PROTECTED	20. Keep safe; guarded

Holes Vocabulary Fill In The Blanks 3

1. Delicious, invigorating drink
2. Very tired; weary
3. Smothering; suffocating
4. Found guilty
5. Floating or suspended in air
6. Put off until another time
7. Changed to vapor
8. Draw away from something surprising or painful
9. Mentally confused
10. Systematic examination
11. Embarrassing; being disgraced
12. Writing paper and envelopes
13. Something that is an element; a part of
14. Able to be seen
15. Heavier or larger on one side than the other
16. Shut in; confined--usually in jail
17. Refuses to yield
18. Sticking out; jutting out
19. Spider-like animal with a venomous tail
20. Stolen goods

Holes Vocabulary Fill In The Blanks 3 Answer Key

NECTAR	1. Delicious, invigorating drink
EXHAUSTED	2. Very tired; weary
STIFLING	3. Smothering; suffocating
CONDEMNED	4. Found guilty
HOVER	5. Floating or suspended in air
DELAYED	6. Put off until another time
EVAPORATED	7. Changed to vapor
FLINCH	8. Draw away from something surprising or painful
DELIRIOUS	9. Mentally confused
INVESTIGATION	10. Systematic examination
HUMILIATING	11. Embarrassing; being disgraced
STATIONERY	12. Writing paper and envelopes
INGREDIENT	13. Something that is an element; a part of
VISIBLE	14. Able to be seen
LOPSIDED	15. Heavier or larger on one side than the other
INCARCERATED	16. Shut in; confined--usually in jail
INSISTS	17. Refuses to yield
PROTRUDING	18. Sticking out; jutting out
SCORPION	19. Spider-like animal with a venomous tail
LOOT	20. Stolen goods

Holes Vocabulary Fill In The Blanks 4

_____   1. Not giving up

_____   2. Found guilty

_____   3. Reproduction of the form of something or someone

_____   4. Poisonous secretion of an animal, such as a spider or snake

_____   5. Draw away from something surprising or painful

_____   6. Spread out in straggling or disorderly fashion

_____   7. Forced out

_____   8. Dreary; unfit for habitation or use

_____   9. Condemned to a severe penalty

_____   10. Shut in; confined--usually in jail

_____   11. Keep safe; guarded

_____   12. Appeals for evil or injury to befall someone or something

_____   13. Smothering; suffocating

_____   14. Having a thickening and hardness of skin

_____   15. Vile; awful

_____   16. Place of protection or shelter

_____   17. Jargon formed by putting first consonant at the end of a word and adding a syllable: ___ Latin

_____   18. Get better

_____   19. Soaked with moisture

_____   20. Absurd; ridiculous

Holes Vocabulary Fill In The Blanks 4 Answer Key

PERSEVERANCE	1. Not giving up
CONDEMNED	2. Found guilty
IMAGE	3. Reproduction of the form of something or someone
VENOM	4. Poisonous secretion of an animal, such as a spider or snake
FLINCH	5. Draw away from something surprising or painful
SPRAWLED	6. Spread out in straggling or disorderly fashion
SPEWED	7. Forced out
DESOLATE	8. Dreary; unfit for habitation or use
DOOMED	9. Condemned to a severe penalty
INCARCERATED	10. Shut in; confined--usually in jail
PROTECTED	11. Keep safe; guarded
CURSES	12. Appeals for evil or injury to befall someone or something
STIFLING	13. Smothering; suffocating
CALLUSED	14. Having a thickening and hardness of skin
DESPICABLE	15. Vile; awful
REFUGE	16. Place of protection or shelter
PIG	17. Jargon formed by putting first consonant at the end of a word and adding a syllable: ____ Latin
IMPROVE	18. Get better
SOGGY	19. Soaked with moisture
PREPOSTEROUS	20. Absurd; ridiculous

Holes Vocabulary Matching 1

___ 1. PROTECTED   A. Outlandish; bizarre
___ 2. GULLY   B. Mentally confused
___ 3. DREAD   C. Necessary things
___ 4. FOSSIL   D. Clumsy; unskillful
___ 5. GROTESQUE   E. Like or containing a metal
___ 6. CAUTIOUS   F. Sterile; dull; unfruitful
___ 7. RATIO   G. Got smaller
___ 8. BARREN   H. Keep safe; guarded
___ 9. LOPSIDED   I. Jargon formed by putting first consonant at the end of a word and adding a syllable: ___ Latin
___10. STATIONERY   J. Consistent in reasoning
___11. FUGITIVE   K. Careful
___12. PIG   L. Hooking to; connecting
___13. FIERY   M. Writing paper and envelopes
___14. SHRANK   N. Place of protection or shelter
___15. THROBBING   O. Poisonous secretion of an animal, such as a spider or snake
___16. AWKWARD   P. Skeleton or imprint of an organism in a rock
___17. LOGICAL   Q. Very hot; like fire
___18. STIFLING   R. Smothering; suffocating
___19. REQUIREMENTS   S. Area of authority or control
___20. METALLIC   T. Heavier or larger on one side than the other
___21. VENOM   U. Beating rapidly or violently; pounding
___22. REFUGE   V. Deep ditch cut in the earth by running water
___23. DELIRIOUS   W. Person running away from the law
___24. JURISDICTION   X. Anticipate with fear, alarm, or reluctance
___25. HITCHING   Y. Relation between two things

Holes Vocabulary Matching 1 Answer Key

H - 1. PROTECTED
V - 2. GULLY
X - 3. DREAD
P - 4. FOSSIL
A - 5. GROTESQUE
K - 6. CAUTIOUS
Y - 7. RATIO
F - 8. BARREN
T - 9. LOPSIDED
M -10. STATIONERY
W -11. FUGITIVE
I - 12. PIG
Q -13. FIERY
G -14. SHRANK
U -15. THROBBING
D -16. AWKWARD
J - 17. LOGICAL
R -18. STIFLING
C -19. REQUIREMENTS
E -20. METALLIC
O -21. VENOM
N -22. REFUGE
B -23. DELIRIOUS
S -24. JURISDICTION
L -25. HITCHING

A. Outlandish; bizarre
B. Mentally confused
C. Necessary things
D. Clumsy; unskillful
E. Like or containing a metal
F. Sterile; dull; unfruitful
G. Got smaller
H. Keep safe; guarded
I. Jargon formed by putting first consonant at the end of a word and adding a syllable: ___ Latin
J. Consistent in reasoning
K. Careful
L. Hooking to; connecting
M. Writing paper and envelopes
N. Place of protection or shelter
O. Poisonous secretion of an animal, such as a spider or snake
P. Skeleton or imprint of an organism in a rock
Q. Very hot; like fire
R. Smothering; suffocating
S. Area of authority or control
T. Heavier or larger on one side than the other
U. Beating rapidly or violently; pounding
V. Deep ditch cut in the earth by running water
W. Person running away from the law
X. Anticipate with fear, alarm, or reluctance
Y. Relation between two things

Holes Vocabulary Matching 2

___ 1. EVAPORATED   A. Soaked with moisture
___ 2. CALLUSED   B. Shut in; confined--usually in jail
___ 3. PRECARIOUS   C. Relation between two things
___ 4. PRECIPICE   D. Extremely steep or overhanging mass of rock
___ 5. DESOLATE   E. Consistent in reasoning
___ 6. SCORPION   F. Having a thickening and hardness of skin
___ 7. WASTELAND   G. Heavier or larger on one side than the other
___ 8. FABULOUS   H. Sterile; dull; unfruitful
___ 9. REQUIREMENTS   I. Have doubts about; distrust
___ 10. EXHAUSTED   J. Filled with surprise; astonished
___ 11. SOGGY   K. Dangerously lacking in security or stability
___ 12. FUGITIVE   L. Very tired; weary
___ 13. LOGICAL   M. Person running away from the law
___ 14. URGE   N. Necessary things
___ 15. BARREN   O. Uncultivated or desolate country
___ 16. MYSTERIOUS   P. Carved, cut, or etched into something
___ 17. SUSPECT   Q. Changed to vapor
___ 18. AMAZED   R. Dreary; unfit for habitation or use
___ 19. VENTILATION   S. Admitting fresh air to replace stale air
___ 20. RATIO   T. Barely believable; astonishing; amazing
___ 21. ENGRAVED   U. Appeals for evil or injury to befall someone or something
___ 22. CURSES   V. Spider-like animal with a venomous tail
___ 23. INCARCERATED   W. Individuals from which others come; opposite of ancestors
___ 24. DESCENDANTS   X. Not fully understood
___ 25. LOPSIDED   Y. Force moving one to do something

Holes Vocabulary Matching 2 Answer Key

Q - 1.	EVAPORATED	A.	Soaked with moisture
F - 2.	CALLUSED	B.	Shut in; confined--usually in jail
K - 3.	PRECARIOUS	C.	Relation between two things
D - 4.	PRECIPICE	D.	Extremely steep or overhanging mass of rock
R - 5.	DESOLATE	E.	Consistent in reasoning
V - 6.	SCORPION	F.	Having a thickening and hardness of skin
O - 7.	WASTELAND	G.	Heavier or larger on one side than the other
T - 8.	FABULOUS	H.	Sterile; dull; unfruitful
N - 9.	REQUIREMENTS	I.	Have doubts about; distrust
L - 10.	EXHAUSTED	J.	Filled with surprise; astonished
A - 11.	SOGGY	K.	Dangerously lacking in security or stability
M - 12.	FUGITIVE	L.	Very tired; weary
E - 13.	LOGICAL	M.	Person running away from the law
Y - 14.	URGE	N.	Necessary things
H - 15.	BARREN	O.	Uncultivated or desolate country
X - 16.	MYSTERIOUS	P.	Carved, cut, or etched into something
I - 17.	SUSPECT	Q.	Changed to vapor
J - 18.	AMAZED	R.	Dreary; unfit for habitation or use
S - 19.	VENTILATION	S.	Admitting fresh air to replace stale air
C - 20.	RATIO	T.	Barely believable; astonishing; amazing
P - 21.	ENGRAVED	U.	Appeals for evil or injury to befall someone or something
U - 22.	CURSES	V.	Spider-like animal with a venomous tail
B - 23.	INCARCERATED	W.	Individuals from which others come; opposite of ancestors
W - 24.	DESCENDANTS	X.	Not fully understood
G - 25.	LOPSIDED	Y.	Force moving one to do something

Holes Vocabulary Matching 3

___ 1. DOOMED	A. Got smaller
___ 2. JURISDICTION	B. Refuses to yield
___ 3. HITCHING	C. Outlandish; bizarre
___ 4. ADJACENT	D. Very tired; weary
___ 5. HUMILIATING	E. Vile; awful
___ 6. SOGGY	F. Not able to be explained or interpreted
___ 7. FIERY	G. Condemned to a severe penalty
___ 8. SHRANK	H. Beating rapidly or violently; pounding
___ 9. THROBBING	I. Keep safe; guarded
___10. DEFECTIVE	J. Understand
___11. FLINCH	K. Filled with surprise; astonished
___12. PARCHED	L. Very hot; like fire
___13. GROTESQUE	M. Very dry
___14. COMPREHEND	N. Area of authority or control
___15. SWISH	O. Flawed; doesn't work right
___16. INSISTS	P. Soaked with moisture
___17. CURSES	Q. Lacking strength
___18. FEEBLE	R. Close together; next to
___19. AMAZED	S. Embarrassing; being disgraced
___20. HAZE	T. Hooking to; connecting
___21. DELIRIOUS	U. Mentally confused
___22. DESPICABLE	V. Draw away from something surprising or painful
___23. INEXPLICABLE	W. Moisture, dust, or vapor suspended in the air
___24. PROTECTED	X. Appeals for evil or injury to befall someone or something
___25. EXHAUSTED	Y. Move with a whistle or hiss

HHoles Vocabulary Matching 3 Answer Key

G - 1.	DOOMED	A.	Got smaller
N - 2.	JURISDICTION	B.	Refuses to yield
T - 3.	HITCHING	C.	Outlandish; bizarre
R - 4.	ADJACENT	D.	Very tired; weary
S - 5.	HUMILIATING	E.	Vile; awful
P - 6.	SOGGY	F.	Not able to be explained or interpreted
L - 7.	FIERY	G.	Condemned to a severe penalty
A - 8.	SHRANK	H.	Beating rapidly or violently; pounding
H - 9.	THROBBING	I.	Keep safe; guarded
O - 10.	DEFECTIVE	J.	Understand
V - 11.	FLINCH	K.	Filled with surprise; astonished
M - 12.	PARCHED	L.	Very hot; like fire
C - 13.	GROTESQUE	M.	Very dry
J - 14.	COMPREHEND	N.	Area of authority or control
Y - 15.	SWISH	O.	Flawed; doesn't work right
B - 16.	INSISTS	P.	Soaked with moisture
X - 17.	CURSES	Q.	Lacking strength
Q - 18.	FEEBLE	R.	Close together; next to
K - 19.	AMAZED	S.	Embarrassing; being disgraced
W - 20.	HAZE	T.	Hooking to; connecting
U - 21.	DELIRIOUS	U.	Mentally confused
E - 22.	DESPICABLE	V.	Draw away from something surprising or painful
F - 23.	INEXPLICABLE	W.	Moisture, dust, or vapor suspended in the air
I - 24.	PROTECTED	X.	Appeals for evil or injury to befall someone or something
D - 25.	EXHAUSTED	Y.	Move with a whistle or hiss

HHoles Vocabulary Matching 4

___ 1. INGREDIENT
___ 2. SUSPECT
___ 3. VENTILATION
___ 4. SPRAWLED
___ 5. MIRAGE
___ 6. PIG
___ 7. INEXPLICABLE
___ 8. JURISDICTION
___ 9. HAZE
___10. GROTESQUE
___11. HOVER
___12. DOOMED
___13. CALLUSED
___14. PERSEVERANCE
___15. PRECARIOUS
___16. LOGICAL
___17. MYSTERIOUS
___18. THROBBING
___19. DREAD
___20. URGE
___21. SUBTLE
___22. SCARCITY
___23. COMPREHEND
___24. DESCENDANTS
___25. SPEWED

A. Not fully understood
B. Moisture, dust, or vapor suspended in the air
C. Condemned to a severe penalty
D. Outlandish; bizarre
E. Jargon formed by putting first consonant at the end of a word and adding a syllable: ___ Latin
F. Not giving up
G. Beating rapidly or violently; pounding
H. Dangerously lacking in security or stability
I. Not able to be explained or interpreted
J. Spread out in straggling or disorderly fashion
K. Consistent in reasoning
L. Floating or suspended in air
M. Something that is an element; a part of
N. Forced out
O. An illusion; something deceptive
P. So slight as to be difficult to distinguish
Q. Having a thickening and hardness of skin
R. Anticipate with fear, alarm, or reluctance
S. Force moving one to do something
T. Shortage
U. Understand
V. Admitting fresh air to replace stale air
W. Area of authority or control
X. Have doubts about; distrust
Y. Individuals from which others come; opposite of ancestors

HHoles Vocabulary Matching 4 Answer Key

M - 1. INGREDIENT   A. Not fully understood
X - 2. SUSPECT   B. Moisture, dust, or vapor suspended in the air
V - 3. VENTILATION   C. Condemned to a severe penalty
J - 4. SPRAWLED   D. Outlandish; bizarre
O - 5. MIRAGE   E. Jargon formed by putting first consonant at the end of a word and adding a syllable: ___ Latin
E - 6. PIG   F. Not giving up
I - 7. INEXPLICABLE   G. Beating rapidly or violently; pounding
W - 8. JURISDICTION   H. Dangerously lacking in security or stability
B - 9. HAZE   I. Not able to be explained or interpreted
D - 10. GROTESQUE   J. Spread out in straggling or disorderly fashion
L - 11. HOVER   K. Consistent in reasoning
C - 12. DOOMED   L. Floating or suspended in air
Q - 13. CALLUSED   M. Something that is an element; a part of
F - 14. PERSEVERANCE   N. Forced out
H - 15. PRECARIOUS   O. An illusion; something deceptive
K - 16. LOGICAL   P. So slight as to be difficult to distinguish
A - 17. MYSTERIOUS   Q. Having a thickening and hardness of skin
G - 18. THROBBING   R. Anticipate with fear, alarm, or reluctance
R - 19. DREAD   S. Force moving one to do something
S - 20. URGE   T. Shortage
P - 21. SUBTLE   U. Understand
T - 22. SCARCITY   V. Admitting fresh air to replace stale air
U - 23. COMPREHEND   W. Area of authority or control
Y - 24. DESCENDANTS   X. Have doubts about; distrust
N - 25. SPEWED   Y. Individuals from which others come; opposite of ancestors

Holes Vocabulary Magic Squares 1

Match the definition with the vocabulary word. Put your answers in the magic squares below. When your answers are correct, all columns and rows will add to the same number.

A. SWISH
B. SOGGY
C. STATIONERY
D. IMAGE
E. FIERY
F. SCARCITY
G. SPRAWLED
H. FOSSIL
I. PREPOSTEROUS
J. GROTESQUE
K. CAUTIOUS
L. PRECARIOUS
M. SHRANK
N. DESOLATE
O. DESPICABLE
P. LOPSIDED

1. Got smaller
2. Shortage
3. Skeleton or imprint of an organism in a rock
4. Vile; awful
5. Dangerously lacking in security or stability
6. Writing paper and envelopes
7. Move with a whistle or hiss
8. Outlandish; bizarre
9. Careful
10. Reproduction of the form of something or someone
11. Soaked with moisture
12. Absurd; ridiculous
13. Dreary; unfit for habitation or use
14. Very hot; like fire
15. Spread out in straggling or disorderly fashion
16. Heavier or larger on one side than the other

A=	B=	C=	D=
E=	F=	G=	H=
I=	J=	K=	L=
M=	N=	O=	P=

Holes Vocabulary Magic Squares 1 Answer Key

Match the definition with the vocabulary word. Put your answers in the magic squares below. When your answers are correct, all columns and rows will add to the same number.

A. SWISH
B. SOGGY
C. STATIONERY
D. IMAGE
E. FIERY
F. SCARCITY
G. SPRAWLED
H. FOSSIL
I. PREPOSTEROUS
J. GROTESQUE
K. CAUTIOUS
L. PRECARIOUS
M. SHRANK
N. DESOLATE
O. DESPICABLE
P. LOPSIDED

1. Got smaller
2. Shortage
3. Skeleton or imprint of an organism in a rock
4. Vile; awful
5. Dangerously lacking in security or stability
6. Writing paper and envelopes
7. Move with a whistle or hiss
8. Outlandish; bizarre
9. Careful
10. Reproduction of the form of something or someone
11. Soaked with moisture
12. Absurd; ridiculous
13. Dreary; unfit for habitation or use
14. Very hot; like fire
15. Spread out in straggling or disorderly fashion
16. Heavier or larger on one side than the other

A=7	B=11	C=6	D=10
E=14	F=2	G=15	H=3
I=12	J=8	K=9	L=5
M=1	N=13	O=4	P=16

Holes Vocabulary Magic Squares 2

Match the definition with the vocabulary word. Put your answers in the magic squares below. When your answers are correct, all columns and rows will add to the same number.

A. ENGRAVED
B. DELIRIOUS
C. THROBBING
D. FUGITIVE
E. PIG
F. SUNDIAL
G. CERTAIN
H. PRECIPICE
I. PROTRUDING
J. PARCHED
K. INVESTIGATION
L. VENOM
M. DESPICABLE
N. PRECARIOUS
O. AMAZED
P. IMPROVE

1. Instrument that indicates local solar time
2. Sticking out; jutting out
3. Filled with surprise; astonished
4. Person running away from the law
5. Vile; awful
6. Mentally confused
7. Extremely steep or overhanging mass of rock
8. Systematic examination
9. Beating rapidly or violently; pounding
10. Get better
11. Very dry
12. Jargon formed by putting first consonant at the end of a word and adding a syllable: ___ Latin
13. Poisonous secretion of an animal, such as a spider or snake
14. Sure
15. Carved, cut, or etched into something
16. Dangerously lacking in security or stability

A=	B=	C=	D=
E=	F=	G=	H=
I=	J=	K=	L=
M=	N=	O=	P=

Holes Vocabulary Magic Squares 2 Answer Key

Match the definition with the vocabulary word. Put your answers in the magic squares below. When your answers are correct, all columns and rows will add to the same number.

A. ENGRAVED
B. DELIRIOUS
C. THROBBING
D. FUGITIVE
E. PIG
F. SUNDIAL
G. CERTAIN
H. PRECIPICE
I. PROTRUDING
J. PARCHED
K. INVESTIGATION
L. VENOM
M. DESPICABLE
N. PRECARIOUS
O. AMAZED
P. IMPROVE

1. Instrument that indicates local solar time
2. Sticking out; jutting out
3. Filled with surprise; astonished
4. Person running away from the law
5. Vile; awful
6. Mentally confused
7. Extremely steep or overhanging mass of rock
8. Systematic examination
9. Beating rapidly or violently; pounding
10. Get better
11. Very dry
12. Jargon formed by putting first consonant at the end of a word and adding a syllable: ___ Latin
13. Poisonous secretion of an animal, such as a spider or snake
14. Sure
15. Carved, cut, or etched into something
16. Dangerously lacking in security or stability

A=15	B=6	C=9	D=4
E=12	F=1	G=14	H=7
I=2	J=11	K=8	L=13
M=5	N=16	O=3	P=10

Holes Vocabulary Magic Squares 3

Match the definition with the vocabulary word. Put your answers in the magic squares below. When your answers are correct, all columns and rows will add to the same number.

A. CALLUSED
B. DESPICABLE
C. FOSSIL
D. FAMILIAR
E. PRECIPICE
F. LOGICAL
G. HAZE
H. APPRECIATE
I. HITCHING
J. DEFECTIVE
K. CONDEMNED
L. CERTAIN
M. DELIRIOUS
N. SOGGY
O. SCARCITY
P. STATIONERY

1. Value
2. Mentally confused
3. Vile; awful
4. Found guilty
5. Flawed; doesn't work right
6. Skeleton or imprint of an organism in a rock
7. Writing paper and envelopes
8. Extremely steep or overhanging mass of rock
9. Shortage
10. Consistent in reasoning
11. Hooking to; connecting
12. Often encountered; known
13. Having a thickening and hardness of skin
14. Sure
15. Moisture, dust, or vapor suspended in the air
16. Soaked with moisture

A=	B=	C=	D=
E=	F=	G=	H=
I=	J=	K=	L=
M=	N=	O=	P=

83
Copyrighted

Holes Vocabulary Magic Squares 3 Answer Key

Match the definition with the vocabulary word. Put your answers in the magic squares below. When your answers are correct, all columns and rows will add to the same number.

A. CALLUSED
B. DESPICABLE
C. FOSSIL
D. FAMILIAR
E. PRECIPICE
F. LOGICAL
G. HAZE
H. APPRECIATE
I. HITCHING
J. DEFECTIVE
K. CONDEMNED
L. CERTAIN
M. DELIRIOUS
N. SOGGY
O. SCARCITY
P. STATIONERY

1. Value
2. Mentally confused
3. Vile; awful
4. Found guilty
5. Flawed; doesn't work right
6. Skeleton or imprint of an organism in a rock
7. Writing paper and envelopes
8. Extremely steep or overhanging mass of rock
9. Shortage
10. Consistent in reasoning
11. Hooking to; connecting
12. Often encountered; known
13. Having a thickening and hardness of skin
14. Sure
15. Moisture, dust, or vapor suspended in the air
16. Soaked with moisture

A=13	B=3	C=6	D=12
E=8	F=10	G=15	H=1
I=11	J=5	K=4	L=14
M=2	N=16	O=9	P=7

HHoles Vocabulary Matching 4

___ 1. INGREDIENT   A. Not fully understood
___ 2. SUSPECT   B. Moisture, dust, or vapor suspended in the air
___ 3. VENTILATION   C. Condemned to a severe penalty
___ 4. SPRAWLED   D. Outlandish; bizarre
___ 5. MIRAGE   E. Jargon formed by putting first consonant at the end of a word and adding a syllable: ___ Latin
___ 6. PIG   F. Not giving up
___ 7. INEXPLICABLE   G. Beating rapidly or violently; pounding
___ 8. JURISDICTION   H. Dangerously lacking in security or stability
___ 9. HAZE   I. Not able to be explained or interpreted
___10. GROTESQUE   J. Spread out in straggling or disorderly fashion
___11. HOVER   K. Consistent in reasoning
___12. DOOMED   L. Floating or suspended in air
___13. CALLUSED   M. Something that is an element; a part of
___14. PERSEVERANCE   N. Forced out
___15. PRECARIOUS   O. An illusion; something deceptive
___16. LOGICAL   P. So slight as to be difficult to distinguish
___17. MYSTERIOUS   Q. Having a thickening and hardness of skin
___18. THROBBING   R. Anticipate with fear, alarm, or reluctance
___19. DREAD   S. Force moving one to do something
___20. URGE   T. Shortage
___21. SUBTLE   U. Understand
___22. SCARCITY   V. Admitting fresh air to replace stale air
___23. COMPREHEND   W. Area of authority or control
___24. DESCENDANTS   X. Have doubts about; distrust
___25. SPEWED   Y. Individuals from which others come; opposite of ancestors

HHoles Vocabulary Matching 4 Answer Key

M - 1.	INGREDIENT	A.	Not fully understood
X - 2.	SUSPECT	B.	Moisture, dust, or vapor suspended in the air
V - 3.	VENTILATION	C.	Condemned to a severe penalty
J - 4.	SPRAWLED	D.	Outlandish; bizarre
O - 5.	MIRAGE	E.	Jargon formed by putting first consonant at the end of a word and adding a syllable: ___ Latin
E - 6.	PIG	F.	Not giving up
I - 7.	INEXPLICABLE	G.	Beating rapidly or violently; pounding
W - 8.	JURISDICTION	H.	Dangerously lacking in security or stability
B - 9.	HAZE	I.	Not able to be explained or interpreted
D - 10.	GROTESQUE	J.	Spread out in straggling or disorderly fashion
L - 11.	HOVER	K.	Consistent in reasoning
C - 12.	DOOMED	L.	Floating or suspended in air
Q - 13.	CALLUSED	M.	Something that is an element; a part of
F - 14.	PERSEVERANCE	N.	Forced out
H - 15.	PRECARIOUS	O.	An illusion; something deceptive
K - 16.	LOGICAL	P.	So slight as to be difficult to distinguish
A - 17.	MYSTERIOUS	Q.	Having a thickening and hardness of skin
G - 18.	THROBBING	R.	Anticipate with fear, alarm, or reluctance
R - 19.	DREAD	S.	Force moving one to do something
S - 20.	URGE	T.	Shortage
P - 21.	SUBTLE	U.	Understand
T - 22.	SCARCITY	V.	Admitting fresh air to replace stale air
U - 23.	COMPREHEND	W.	Area of authority or control
Y - 24.	DESCENDANTS	X.	Have doubts about; distrust
N - 25.	SPEWED	Y.	Individuals from which others come; opposite of ancestors

Holes Vocabulary Word Search 1

Words are placed backwards, forward, diagonally, up and down. Clues listed below can help you find the words. Circle the hidden vocabulary words in the maze.

```
S O G G Y Y T I C R A C S P S F J A C S
U B S N H Z N I M L A D U I P L U M O C
O A U I B O L N I A C T O G R I R A N M
L R B H E L V S Z C G T I M A N I Z D R
U R T C A X S E M U D E R O W C S E E G
B E L T Q O H S R R W L I N L H D D M F
A N E I F K T A J S R D L E E B I A N Z
F M M H E C L W U E E H E V D C C D E J
M Y S T E R I O U S S Y D P E H T J D X
K E X P B B Y Y O T T A R R V S I A D Q
D G S W L R T L S T E E K H A I O C R S
S U R G E P A I R R C S D X R W N E A S
S F W I Z T S P D I D P G H G S L N W P
N E F X E N N T P V P E B A N U D T K M
M R S T I F L I N G M W P Z E T L B W X
P I N C A R C E R A T E D E S U L L A C
T N E I D E R G N I B D E L A Y E D Y L
```

Anticipate with fear, alarm, or reluctance (5)
Appeals for evil or injury to befall someone or something (6)
Area of authority or control (12)
Barely believable; astonishing; amazing (8)
Carved, cut, or etched into something (8)
Close together; next to (8)
Clumsy; unskillful (7)
Deep ditch cut in the earth by running water (5)
Delicious, invigorating drink (6)
Draw away from something surprising or painful (6)
Dreary; unfit for habitation or use (8)
Extremely steep or overhanging mass of rock (9)
Filled with surprise; astonished (6)
Floating or suspended in air (5)
Force moving one to do something (4)
Forced out (6)
Found guilty (9)
Have doubts about; distrust (7)
Having a thickening and hardness of skin (8)
Hooking to; connecting (8)
Jargon formed by putting first consonant at the end of a word and adding a syllable: ___ Latin (3)
Lacking strength (6)
Like or containing a metal (8)

Mentally confused (9)
Moisture, dust, or vapor suspended in the air (4)
Move with a whistle or hiss (5)
Not fully understood (10)
Place of protection or shelter (6)
Poisonous secretion of an animal, such as a spider or snake (5)
Put off until another time (7)
Refuses to yield (7)
Relation between two things (5)
Reproduction of the form of something or someone (5)
Shortage (8)
Shut in; confined--usually in jail (12)
Skeleton or imprint of an organism in a rock (6)
Smothering; suffocating (8)
So slight as to be difficult to distinguish (6)
Soaked with moisture (5)
Something that is an element; a part of (10)
Speech characterized by lengthened, drawn-out vowels (5)
Spread out in straggling or disorderly fashion (8)
Sterile; dull; unfruitful (6)
Stolen goods (4)
Very hot; like fire (5)
Very tired; weary (9)

Holes Vocabulary Word Search 1 Answer Key

Words are placed backwards, forward, diagonally, up and down. Clues listed below can help you find the words. Circle the hidden vocabulary words in the maze.

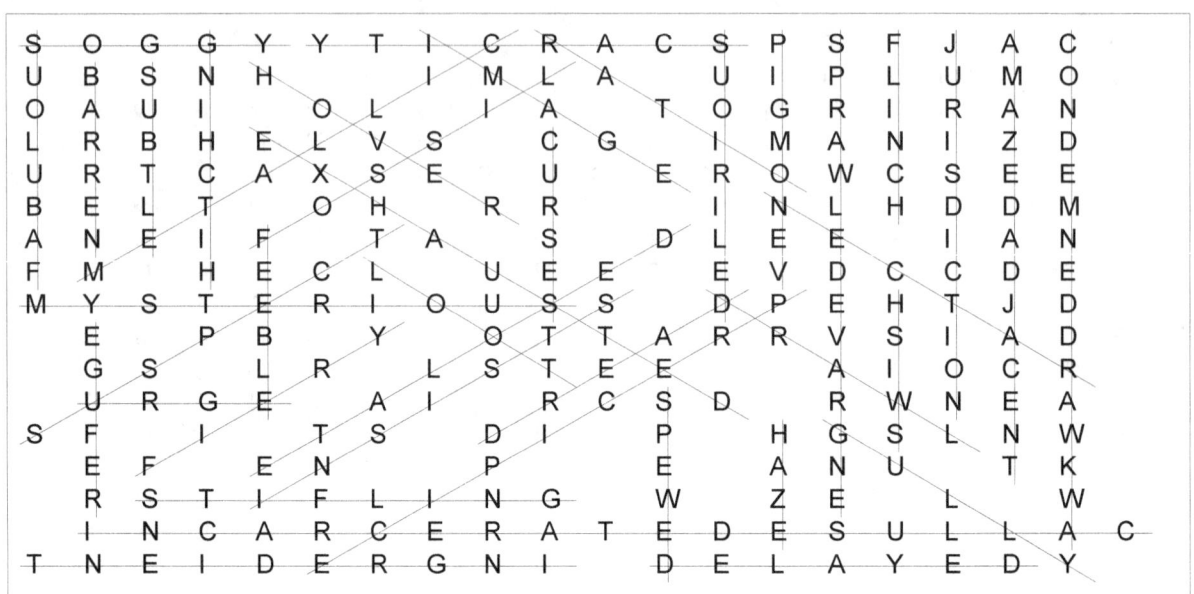

Anticipate with fear, alarm, or reluctance (5)
Appeals for evil or injury to befall someone or something (6)
Area of authority or control (12)
Barely believable; astonishing; amazing (8)
Carved, cut, or etched into something (8)
Close together; next to (8)
Clumsy; unskillful (7)
Deep ditch cut in the earth by running water (5)
Delicious, invigorating drink (6)
Draw away from something surprising or painful (6)
Dreary; unfit for habitation or use (8)
Extremely steep or overhanging mass of rock (9)
Filled with surprise; astonished (6)
Floating or suspended in air (5)
Force moving one to do something (4)
Forced out (6)
Found guilty (9)
Have doubts about; distrust (7)
Having a thickening and hardness of skin (8)
Hooking to; connecting (8)
Jargon formed by putting first consonant at the end of a word and adding a syllable: ___ Latin (3)
Lacking strength (6)
Like or containing a metal (8)

Mentally confused (9)
Moisture, dust, or vapor suspended in the air (4)
Move with a whistle or hiss (5)
Not fully understood (10)
Place of protection or shelter (6)
Poisonous secretion of an animal, such as a spider or snake (5)
Put off until another time (7)
Refuses to yield (7)
Relation between two things (5)
Reproduction of the form of something or someone (5)
Shortage (8)
Shut in; confined--usually in jail (12)
Skeleton or imprint of an organism in a rock (6)
Smothering; suffocating (8)
So slight as to be difficult to distinguish (6)
Soaked with moisture (5)
Something that is an element; a part of (10)
Speech characterized by lengthened, drawn-out vowels (5)
Spread out in straggling or disorderly fashion (8)
Sterile; dull; unfruitful (6)
Stolen goods (4)
Very hot; like fire (5)
Very tired; weary (9)

Holes Vocabulary Word Search 2

Words are placed backwards, forward, diagonally, up and down. Clues listed below can help you find the words. Circle the hidden vocabulary words in the maze.

```
D E H T I R W I N E X P L I C A B L E Y
W R F D R V H F E T L G U L L Y A O C L
B G E N Z L P I C A H O F L G F R G T Y
S H R A N K G E T L A R O E G A R I M X
G P P L D I N R A O Z B S T N M E C L G
N R E E P M I Y R S E Q S D I I N A W Q
D E R T R P L L L E H S I E B L D L A D
E C S S E R F H E D C I L L B I E G R U
S I E A F O I B B G N B C A O A T D D J
C P V W U V T G L S I V G Y R R A E F W
E I E K G E S O I S L T G E H A R V L H
N C R W E Z P S I A F B I D T T O A M D
D E A A T S T V I V E G A M I I P R S M
A L N R I S Q D E W E P S Z A O A G O Z
N T C D M B N R S U B T L E C T V N G F
T C E P S U S A P P R E C I A T E E G C
S D S H S I W S E S R U C H O V E R Y F
```

Able to be seen (7)
An illusion; something deceptive (6)
Anticipate with fear, alarm, or reluctance (5)
Appeals for evil or injury to befall someone or something (6)
Beating rapidly or violently; pounding (9)
Carved, cut, or etched into something (8)
Changed to vapor (10)
Clumsy; unskillful (7)
Consistent in reasoning (7)
Deep ditch cut in the earth by running water (5)
Delicious, invigorating drink (6)
Draw away from something surprising or painful (6)
Dreary; unfit for habitation or use (8)
Extremely steep or overhanging mass of rock (9)
Floating or suspended in air (5)
Force moving one to do something (4)
Forced out (6)
Get better (7)
Got smaller (6)
Have doubts about; distrust (7)
Heavier or larger on one side than the other (8)
Individuals from which others come; opposite of ancestors (11)
Instrument that indicates local solar time (7)
Jargon formed by putting first consonant at the end of a word and adding a syllable: ___ Latin (3)
Lawful; legal (10)
Moisture, dust, or vapor suspended in the air (4)
Move with a whistle or hiss (5)
Not able to be explained or interpreted (12)
Not giving up (12)
Often encountered; known (8)
Place of protection or shelter (6)
Poisonous secretion of an animal, such as a spider or snake (5)
Put off until another time (7)
Refuses to yield (7)
Relation between two things (5)
Reproduction of the form of something or someone (5)
Skeleton or imprint of an organism in a rock (6)
Smothering; suffocating (8)
So slight as to be difficult to distinguish (6)
Soaked with moisture (5)
Speech characterized by lengthened, drawn-out vowels (5)
Sterile; dull; unfruitful (6)
Stolen goods (4)
Twisted; squirmed (7)
Uncultivated or desolate country (9)
Value (10)
Very hot; like fire (5)

Holes Vocabulary Word Search 2 Answer Key

Words are placed backwards, forward, diagonally, up and down. Clues listed below can help you find the words. Circle the hidden vocabulary words in the maze.

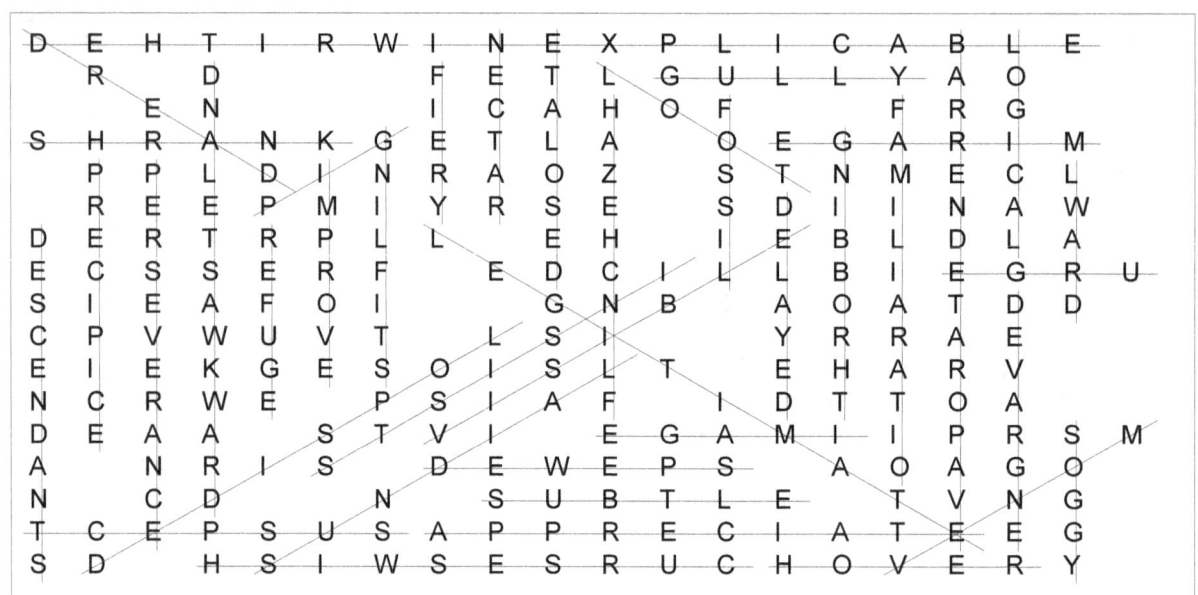

Able to be seen (7)
An illusion; something deceptive (6)
Anticipate with fear, alarm, or reluctance (5)
Appeals for evil or injury to befall someone or something (6)
Beating rapidly or violently; pounding (9)
Carved, cut, or etched into something (8)
Changed to vapor (10)
Clumsy; unskillful (7)
Consistent in reasoning (7)
Deep ditch cut in the earth by running water (5)
Delicious, invigorating drink (6)
Draw away from something surprising or painful (6)
Dreary; unfit for habitation or use (8)
Extremely steep or overhanging mass of rock (9)
Floating or suspended in air (5)
Force moving one to do something (4)
Forced out (6)
Get better (7)
Got smaller (6)
Have doubts about; distrust (7)
Heavier or larger on one side than the other (8)
Individuals from which others come; opposite of ancestors (11)
Instrument that indicates local solar time (7)
Jargon formed by putting first consonant at the end of a word and adding a syllable: ___ Latin

(3)
Lawful; legal (10)
Moisture, dust, or vapor suspended in the air (4)
Move with a whistle or hiss (5)
Not able to be explained or interpreted (12)
Not giving up (12)
Often encountered; known (8)
Place of protection or shelter (6)
Poisonous secretion of an animal, such as a spider or snake (5)
Put off until another time (7)
Refuses to yield (7)
Relation between two things (5)
Reproduction of the form of something or someone (5)
Skeleton or imprint of an organism in a rock (6)
Smothering; suffocating (8)
So slight as to be difficult to distinguish (6)
Soaked with moisture (5)
Speech characterized by lengthened, drawn-out vowels (5)
Sterile; dull; unfruitful (6)
Stolen goods (4)
Twisted; squirmed (7)
Uncultivated or desolate country (9)
Value (10)
Very hot; like fire (5)

Holes Vocabulary Word Search 3

Words are placed backwards, forward, diagonally, up and down. Words listed below are included in the maze. Circle the hidden vocabulary words in the maze.

```
B W R I T H E D D E C I P I C E R P I K
R A T C E N U E E L O D L N U L E R N C
D L R R Y G Q W L B M R H V R B T O S D
K N A R H S S E I I P E G E S E R T I G
L O O T E G E P R S R A D S E E I E S S
N Y I C I N T S I I E D L T S F E C T Z
L J T P Z H O D O V H S W I S H V T S P
X J A K C V R X U X E U A G Y O E E H M
F N R N L A G M S N N O R A J V D D N Z
R T I J W O S F G J D I D T C E Q D D N
S L O K K D G R X Z Y R E I F R E E W D
F O W R E W A I S N T A N O M H D L N Y
R A G Z M V I C C I G C D N C I K A U J
E F A G E E A M D A D E G R S H L R M Q
Z M M D Y R N L P T L R A P V E G I J G
A D J A C E N T P R E P O S T E R O U S
H D L I R E F U G E O L Z S G A N L S R
C Q T L S U S P E C T V A H G P L O J P
S Y H V D O O M E D F W E E X Y R J M C
```

ADJACENT	FEEBLE	LOPSIDED	SCARCITY
AMAZED	FIERY	MIRAGE	SHRANK
AWKWARD	FLINCH	NECTAR	SOGGY
BARREN	GROTESQUE	PARCHED	SPEWED
CERTAIN	GULLY	PIG	SUSPECT
COMPREHEND	HAZE	PRECARIOUS	SWISH
CURSES	HOVER	PRECIPICE	TORMENT
DELIRIOUS	IMPROVE	PREPOSTEROUS	URGE
DOOMED	INSISTS	PROTECTED	VENOM
DRAWL	INVESTIGATION	RATIO	VISIBLE
DREAD	LOGICAL	REFUGE	WASTELAND
ENGRAVED	LOOT	RETRIEVED	WRITHED

Holes Vocabulary Word Search 3 Answer Key

Words are placed backwards, forward, diagonally, up and down. Words listed below are included in the maze. Circle the hidden vocabulary words in the maze.

ADJACENT	FEEBLE	LOPSIDED	SCARCITY
AMAZED	FIERY	MIRAGE	SHRANK
AWKWARD	FLINCH	NECTAR	SOGGY
BARREN	GROTESQUE	PARCHED	SPEWED
CERTAIN	GULLY	PIG	SUSPECT
COMPREHEND	HAZE	PRECARIOUS	SWISH
CURSES	HOVER	PRECIPICE	TORMENT
DELIRIOUS	IMPROVE	PREPOSTEROUS	URGE
DOOMED	INSISTS	PROTECTED	VENOM
DRAWL	INVESTIGATION	RATIO	VISIBLE
DREAD	LOGICAL	REFUGE	WASTELAND
ENGRAVED	LOOT	RETRIEVED	WRITHED

Holes Vocabulary Word Search 4

Words are placed backwards, forward, diagonally, up and down. Words listed below are included in the maze. Circle the hidden vocabulary words in the maze.

```
F A M I L I A R E F U G E E D G U L L Y
C T E D I O U S T G C K L E A N S F I L
E T O R M E N T A A B T W W S I U E S X
R S U S P E C T L R B E K C E H O E S Q
T D A E R D M L O U P W I B S C R B O Q
A C Z R O Q U S S S A L Z Q R T E L F X
I Y A N V S J M E R L Y Y V U I T E W Y
N B T N E C A J D A F L I N C H S I W S
S E C D S X V V T E A L Y G W D O Y H Y
I F C Y C Y H E E C F D G T M R P V L Z
S M Q T V X M A I N D E N D T A E F E M
T O I T A R J G U N O E C H E W R I K R
S G W R Q R O I K S I M R T A L P E P B
T Z M H A L Z P N D T O R H I Z A R V D
D E V A R G N E E X B E J S K V E Y Z Q
E C I P I C E R P B L S D O O M E D E J
G N V S D L G S I J O F U G I T I V E D
R M Q X P N K N K T O X K G A M A Z E D
U Q P Z I E G A M I T B Y Y S H R A N K
```

ADJACENT	ENGRAVED	IMPROVE	SHRANK
AMAZED	EXHAUSTED	INGREDIENT	SOGGY
AWKWARD	FAMILIAR	INSISTS	SPEWED
BARREN	FEEBLE	LOGICAL	SUBTLE
CALLUSED	FIERY	LOOT	SUSPECT
CERTAIN	FLINCH	METALLIC	SWISH
CURSES	FOSSIL	MIRAGE	TEDIOUS
DEFECTIVE	FUGITIVE	NECTAR	THROBBING
DELAYED	GULLY	PIG	TORMENT
DESOLATE	HAZE	PRECIPICE	URGE
DOOMED	HITCHING	PREPOSTEROUS	VENOM
DRAWL	HOVER	RATIO	
DREAD	IMAGE	REFUGE	

Holes Vocabulary Word Search 4 Answer Key

Words are placed backwards, forward, diagonally, up and down. Words listed below are included in the maze. Circle the hidden vocabulary words in the maze.

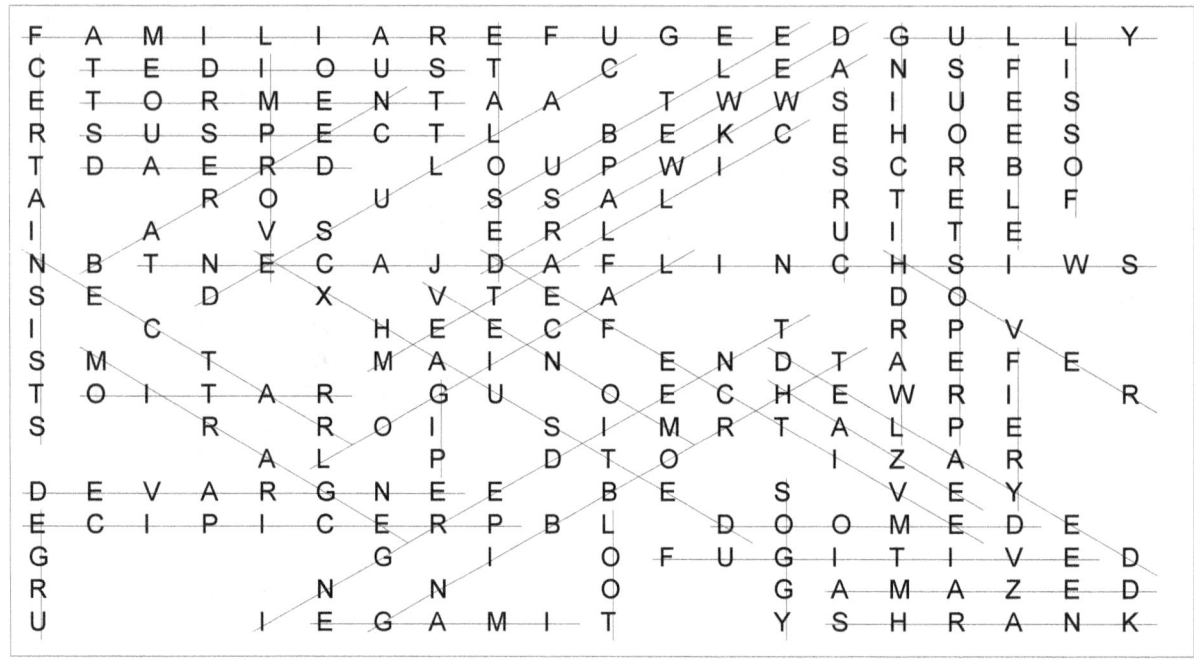

ADJACENT	ENGRAVED	IMPROVE	SHRANK
AMAZED	EXHAUSTED	INGREDIENT	SOGGY
AWKWARD	FAMILIAR	INSISTS	SPEWED
BARREN	FEEBLE	LOGICAL	SUBTLE
CALLUSED	FIERY	LOOT	SUSPECT
CERTAIN	FLINCH	METALLIC	SWISH
CURSES	FOSSIL	MIRAGE	TEDIOUS
DEFECTIVE	FUGITIVE	NECTAR	THROBBING
DELAYED	GULLY	PIG	TORMENT
DESOLATE	HAZE	PRECIPICE	URGE
DOOMED	HITCHING	PREPOSTEROUS	VENOM
DRAWL	HOVER	RATIO	
DREAD	IMAGE	REFUGE	

Holes Vocabulary Crossword 1

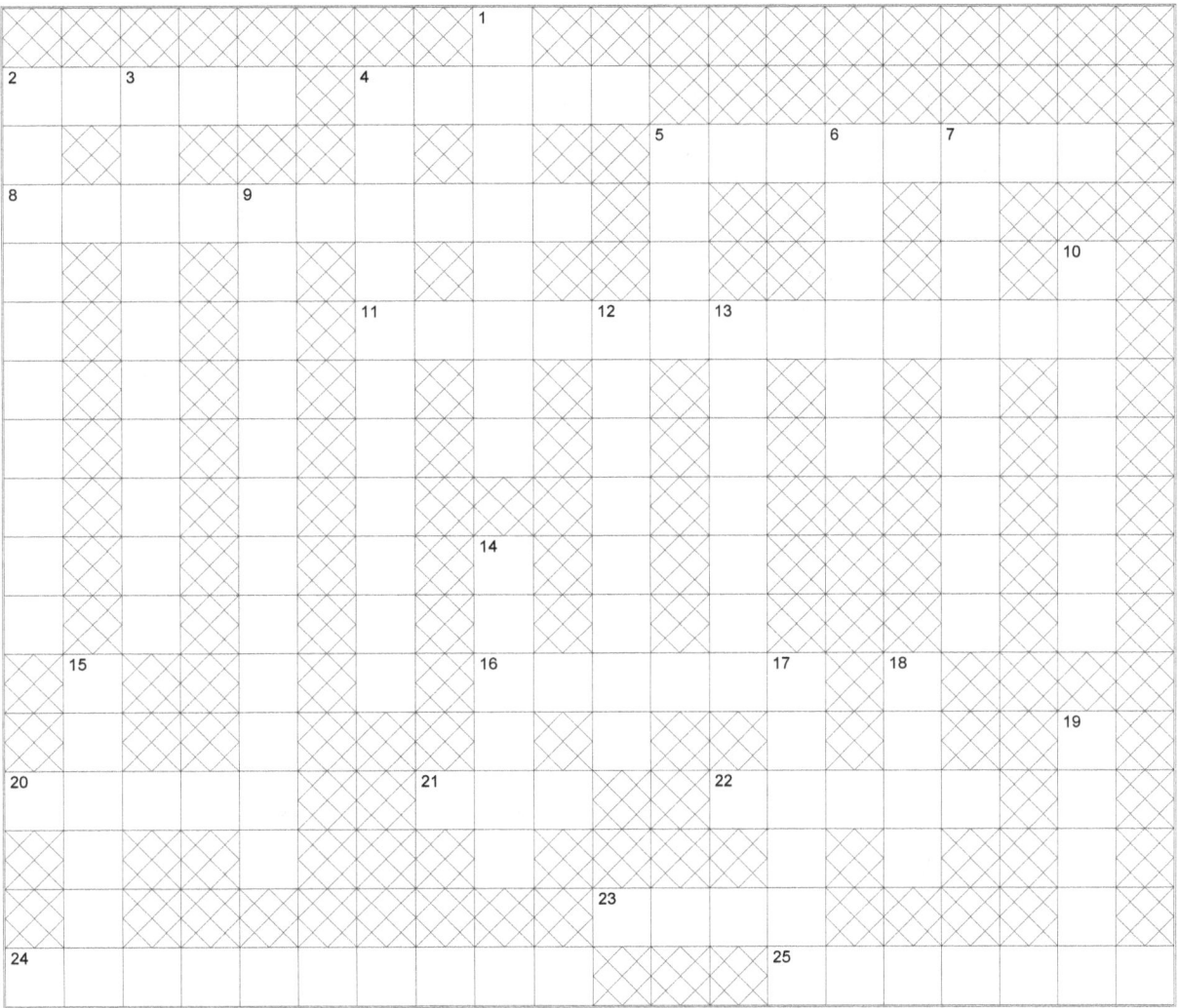

Across
2. Anticipate with fear, alarm, or reluctance
4. Poisonous secretion of an animal, such as a spider or snake
5. Heavier or larger on one side than the other
8. Writing paper and envelopes
11. Systematic examination
16. Forced out
20. Speech characterized by lengthened, drawn-out vowels
21. Jargon formed by putting first consonant at the end of a word and adding a syllable: ___ Latin
22. Soaked with moisture
23. Moisture, dust, or vapor suspended in the air
24. Lawful; legal
25. Put off until another time

Down
1. Carved, cut, or etched into something
2. Vile; awful
3. Changed to vapor
4. Admitting fresh air to replace stale air
5. Stolen goods
6. Got smaller
7. Mentally confused
9. Not able to be explained or interpreted
10. Refuses to yield
12. Spread out in straggling or disorderly fashion
13. Get better
14. Skeleton or imprint of an organism in a rock
15. An illusion; something deceptive
17. Condemned to a severe penalty
18. Force moving one to do something
19. Reproduction of the form of something or someone

Holes Vocabulary Crossword 1 Answer Key

						1							
						E							
2		3			4								
D	R	E	A	D	V	E	N	O	M				
E		V			E		G			5		6		7
										L	O	P	S	I	D	E	D
8				9						O		H		E
S	T	A	T	I	O	N	E	R	Y								10
P		P		N		T		A		O		R		L			I
I		O		E	11				12		13						
					I	N	V	E	S	T	I	G	A	T	I	O	N
C		R		X		L		E	P		M		N		R		S
A		A		P		A		D	R		P		K		I		I
B		T		L		T			A		R				O		S
L		E		I		I	14										
							F		W		O				U		T
E		D		C		O	O		L		V				S		S
	15					16				17		18					
	M		A		N	S	P	E	W	E	D	U					
	I		B			S		D		O		R			19		
20					21				22						I		
D	R	A	W	L	P	I	G		S	O	G	G	Y		M		
	A		E		L				M		E				A		
	G						23								G		
							H	A	Z	E							
24									25								
L	E	G	I	T	I	M	A	T	E	D	E	L	A	Y	E	D	

Across
2. Anticipate with fear, alarm, or reluctance
4. Poisonous secretion of an animal, such as a spider or snake
5. Heavier or larger on one side than the other
8. Writing paper and envelopes
11. Systematic examination
16. Forced out
20. Speech characterized by lengthened, drawn-out vowels
21. Jargon formed by putting first consonant at the end of a word and adding a syllable: ___ Latin
22. Soaked with moisture
23. Moisture, dust, or vapor suspended in the air
24. Lawful; legal
25. Put off until another time

Down
1. Carved, cut, or etched into something
2. Vile; awful
3. Changed to vapor
4. Admitting fresh air to replace stale air
5. Stolen goods
6. Got smaller
7. Mentally confused
9. Not able to be explained or interpreted
10. Refuses to yield
12. Spread out in straggling or disorderly fashion
13. Get better
14. Skeleton or imprint of an organism in a rock
15. An illusion; something deceptive
17. Condemned to a severe penalty
18. Force moving one to do something
19. Reproduction of the form of something or someone

Holes Vocabulary Crossword 2

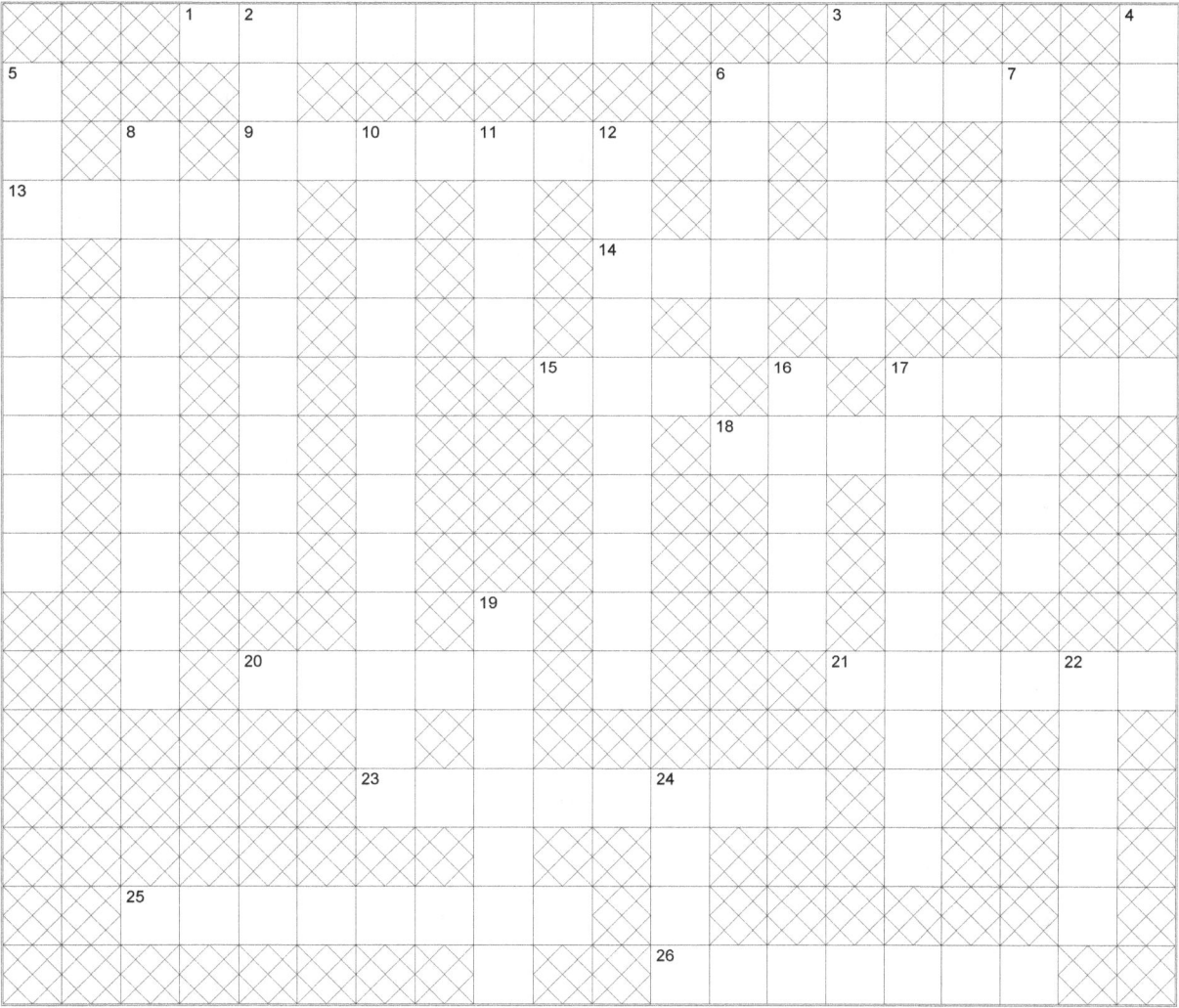

Across
1. Often encountered; known
6. Condemned to a severe penalty
9. Very dry
13. Floating or suspended in air
14. Writing paper and envelopes
15. Jargon formed by putting first consonant at the end of a word and adding a syllable: ___ Latin
17. Relation between two things
18. Force moving one to do something
20. Poisonous secretion of an animal, such as a spider or snake
21. Place of protection or shelter
23. Spread out in straggling or disorderly fashion
25. Person running away from the law
26. Great pain or anguish

Down
2. Value
3. Skeleton or imprint of an organism in a rock
4. Soaked with moisture
5. Very tired; weary
6. Anticipate with fear, alarm, or reluctance
7. Flawed; doesn't work right
8. Changed to vapor
10. Necessary things
11. Moisture, dust, or vapor suspended in the air
12. Vile; awful
16. Speech characterized by lengthened, drawn-out vowels
17. Got back; regained
19. Get better
22. Deep ditch cut in the earth by running water
24. Stolen goods

Holes Vocabulary Crossword 2 Answer Key

Across
1. Often encountered; known
6. Condemned to a severe penalty
9. Very dry
13. Floating or suspended in air
14. Writing paper and envelopes
15. Jargon formed by putting first consonant at the end of a word and adding a syllable: ___ Latin
17. Relation between two things
18. Force moving one to do something
20. Poisonous secretion of an animal, such as a spider or snake
21. Place of protection or shelter
23. Spread out in straggling or disorderly fashion
25. Person running away from the law
26. Great pain or anguish

Down
2. Value
3. Skeleton or imprint of an organism in a rock
4. Soaked with moisture
5. Very tired; weary
6. Anticipate with fear, alarm, or reluctance
7. Flawed; doesn't work right
8. Changed to vapor
10. Necessary things
11. Moisture, dust, or vapor suspended in the air
12. Vile; awful
16. Speech characterized by lengthened, drawn-out vowels
17. Got back; regained
19. Get better
22. Deep ditch cut in the earth by running water
24. Stolen goods

Answers:

Across:
1. FAMILIAR
6. DOOMED
9. PARCHED
13. HOVER
14. STATIONERY
15. PIG
17. RATIO
18. URGE
20. VENOM
21. REFUGE
23. SPRAWLED
25. FUGITIVE
26. TORMENT

Down:
2. IMPORTANCE
3. FOSSIL
4. SOGGY
5. EXHAUSTED
6. DREAD
7. DEFECTIVE
8. EVAPORATED
10. REQUIREMENTS
11. HAZE
12. DESPICABLE
16. DRAWL
17. RETRIEVED
19. IMPROVE
22. GULLY
24. LOOT

Holes Vocabulary Crossword 3

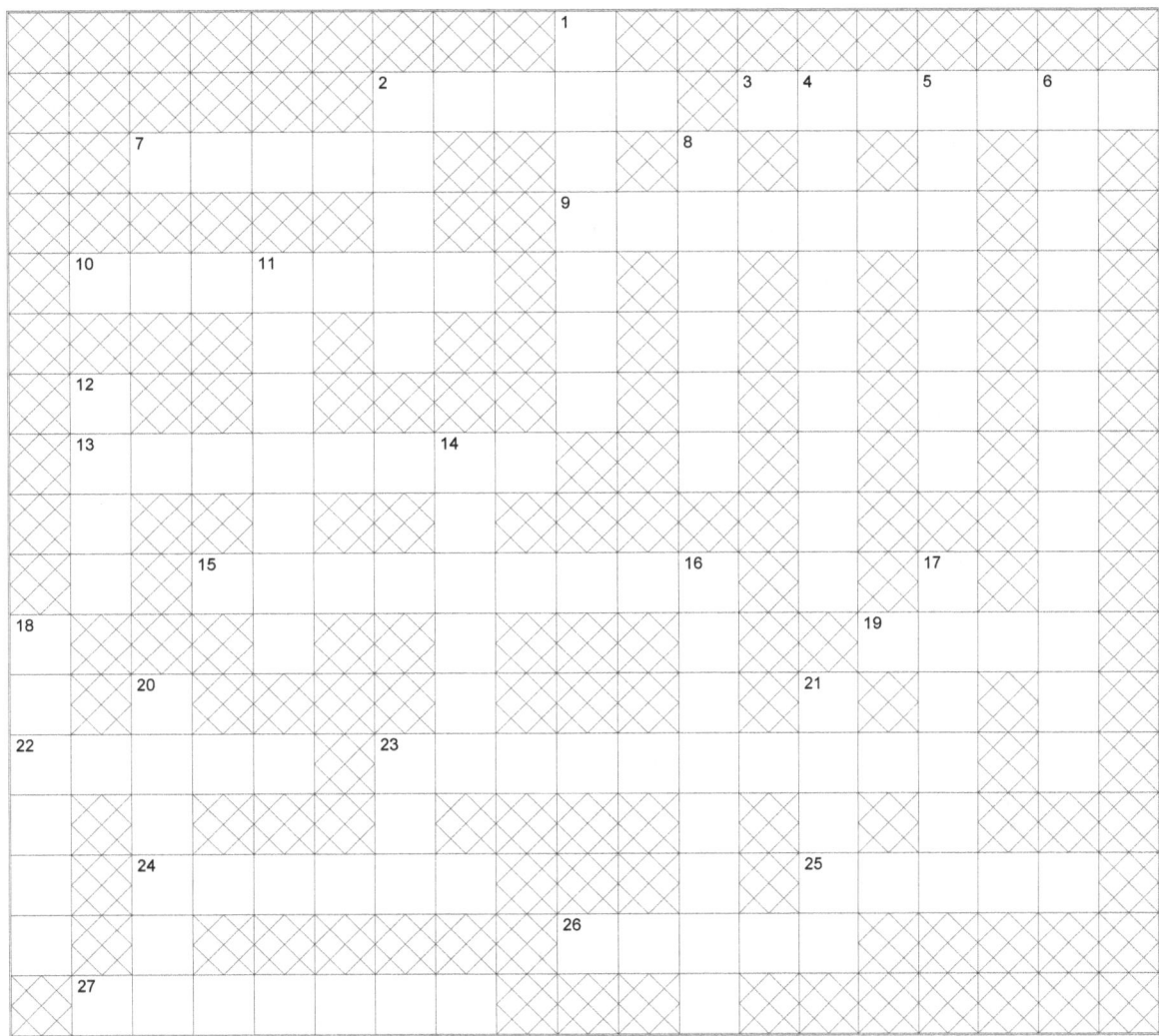

Across
2. Speech characterized by lengthened, drawn-out vowels
3. Sure
7. Floating or suspended in air
9. Twisted; squirmed
10. Instrument that indicates local solar time
13. Close together; next to
15. Flawed; doesn't work right
19. Stolen goods
22. Reproduction of the form of something or someone
23. Dangerously lacking in security or stability
24. Place of protection or shelter
25. Deep ditch cut in the earth by running water
26. Very hot; like fire
27. Refuses to yield

Down
1. Clumsy; unskillful
2. Anticipate with fear, alarm, or reluctance
4. Very tired; weary
5. Tiresome; wearisome
6. Shut in; confined--usually in jail
8. An illusion; something deceptive
11. Put off until another time
12. Moisture, dust, or vapor suspended in the air
14. Delicious, invigorating drink
16. Carved, cut, or etched into something
17. Skeleton or imprint of an organism in a rock
18. Draw away from something surprising or painful
20. Sterile; dull; unfruitful
21. Soaked with moisture
23. Jargon formed by putting first consonant at the end of a word and adding a syllable: ___ Latin

Holes Vocabulary Crossword 3 Answer Key

							1 A						
				2 D	R	A	W	L		3 C	4 E	R	5 T	A	6 I	N
		7 H	O	V	E	R		K		8 M		X		E		N
					E			9 W	R	I	T	H	E	D		C
	10 S	U	11 N	D	I	A	L	A		R		A		I		A
					E		D			R		U		O		R
	12 H		L					D		G		S		U		C
	13 A	D	J	A	C	14 E	N	T		E		T		S		E
	Z				Y		E					E				R
	E		15 D	E	F	E	C	T	I	16 V	E		17 F		A
18 F			D				T			N			19 L	O	O	T
L		20 B					A			G		21 S		S		E
22 I	M	A	G	E		23 P	R	E	C	A	R	I	O	U	S	D
N		R				I				A		G		I	
C	24 R	E	F	U	G	E				V		25 G	U	L	L	Y
H	E					26 F	I	E	R	Y					
	27 I	N	S	I	S	T	S			D					

Across
2. Speech characterized by lengthened, drawn-out vowels
3. Sure
7. Floating or suspended in air
9. Twisted; squirmed
10. Instrument that indicates local solar time
13. Close together; next to
15. Flawed; doesn't work right
19. Stolen goods
22. Reproduction of the form of something or someone
23. Dangerously lacking in security or stability
24. Place of protection or shelter
25. Deep ditch cut in the earth by running water
26. Very hot; like fire
27. Refuses to yield

Down
1. Clumsy; unskillful
2. Anticipate with fear, alarm, or reluctance
4. Very tired; weary
5. Tiresome; wearisome
6. Shut in; confined--usually in jail
8. An illusion; something deceptive
11. Put off until another time
12. Moisture, dust, or vapor suspended in the air
14. Delicious, invigorating drink
16. Carved, cut, or etched into something
17. Skeleton or imprint of an organism in a rock
18. Draw away from something surprising or painful
20. Sterile; dull; unfruitful
21. Soaked with moisture
23. Jargon formed by putting first consonant at the end of a word and adding a syllable: ___ Latin

Holes Vocabulary Crossword 4

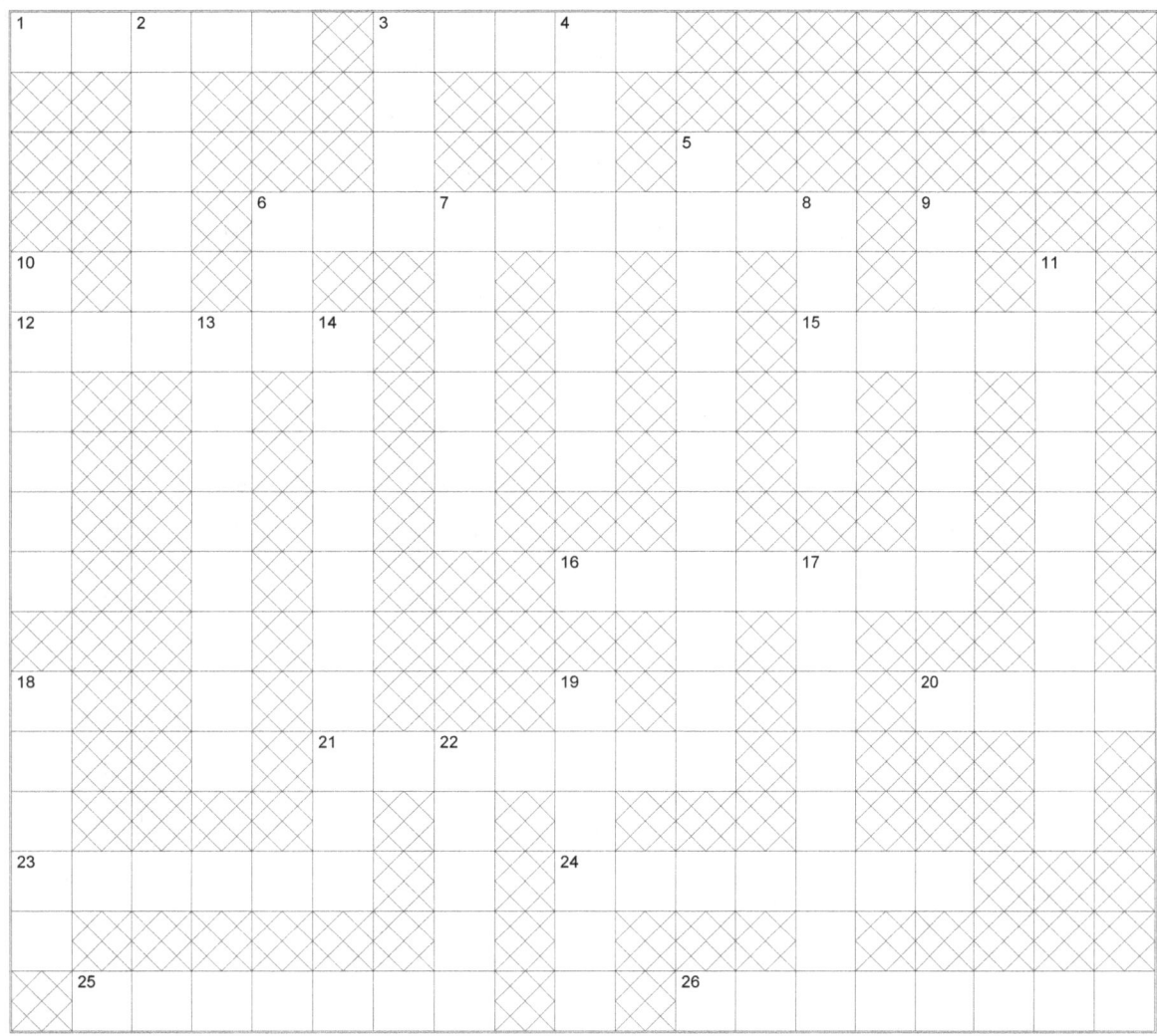

Across
1. Poisonous secretion of an animal, such as a spider or snake
3. Floating or suspended in air
6. Dangerously lacking in security or stability
12. An illusion; something deceptive
15. Deep ditch cut in the earth by running water
16. Twisted; squirmed
20. Stolen goods
21. Tiresome; wearisome
23. Forced out
24. Instrument that indicates local solar time
25. Consistent in reasoning
26. Person running away from the law

Down
2. Delicious, invigorating drink
3. Moisture, dust, or vapor suspended in the air
4. Carved, cut, or etched into something
5. Preparations made by mixing ingredients
6. Jargon formed by putting first consonant at the end of a word and adding a syllable: ___ Latin
7. Appeals for evil or injury to befall someone or something
8. Soaked with moisture
9. Put off until another time
10. Filled with surprise; astonished
11. Not fully understood
13. Close together; next to
14. Changed to vapor
17. Hooking to; connecting
18. Move with a whistle or hiss
19. Skeleton or imprint of an organism in a rock
22. Speech characterized by lengthened, drawn-out vowels

Holes Vocabulary Crossword 4 Answer Key

Across
1. Poisonous secretion of an animal, such as a spider or snake
3. Floating or suspended in air
6. Dangerously lacking in security or stability
12. An illusion; something deceptive
15. Deep ditch cut in the earth by running water
16. Twisted; squirmed
20. Stolen goods
21. Tiresome; wearisome
23. Forced out
24. Instrument that indicates local solar time
25. Consistent in reasoning
26. Person running away from the law

Down
2. Delicious, invigorating drink
3. Moisture, dust, or vapor suspended in the air
4. Carved, cut, or etched into something
5. Preparations made by mixing ingredients
6. Jargon formed by putting first consonant at the end of a word and adding a syllable: ___ Latin
7. Appeals for evil or injury to befall someone or something
8. Soaked with moisture
9. Put off until another time
10. Filled with surprise; astonished
11. Not fully understood
13. Close together; next to
14. Changed to vapor
17. Hooking to; connecting
18. Move with a whistle or hiss
19. Skeleton or imprint of an organism in a rock
22. Speech characterized by lengthened, drawn-out vowels

Holes Vocabulary Juggle Letters 1

1. ODEOMD = 1. _____
   Condemned to a severe penalty

2. ICMETALL = 2. _____
   Like or containing a metal

3. EMOVN = 3. _____
   Poisonous secretion of an animal, such as a spider or snake

4. IARGME = 4. _____
   An illusion; something deceptive

5. AIIRLAMF = 5. _____
   Often encountered; known

6. CCYISRTA = 6. _____
   Shortage

7. IWSSH = 7. _____
   Move with a whistle or hiss

8. DNETEGINRI = 8. _____
   Something that is an element; a part of

9. AMIEG = 9. _____
   Reproduction of the form of something or someone

10. TISNSSI =10. _____
    Refuses to yield

11. TIGVUEIF =11. _____
    Person running away from the law

12. SOIFLS =12. _____
    Skeleton or imprint of an organism in a rock

13. EDLYDAE =13. _____
    Put off until another time

14. GYOGS =14. _____
    Soaked with moisture

15. NITGVEIIOSATN =15. _____
    Systematic examination

Holes Vocabulary Juggle Letters 1 Answer Key

1. ODEOMD = 1. DOOMED
Condemned to a severe penalty

2. ICMETALL = 2. METALLIC
Like or containing a metal

3. EMOVN = 3. VENOM
Poisonous secretion of an animal, such as a spider or snake

4. IARGME = 4. MIRAGE
An illusion; something deceptive

5. AIIRLAMF = 5. FAMILIAR
Often encountered; known

6. CCYISRTA = 6. SCARCITY
Shortage

7. IWSSH = 7. SWISH
Move with a whistle or hiss

8. DNETEGINRI = 8. INGREDIENT
Something that is an element; a part of

9. AMIEG = 9. IMAGE
Reproduction of the form of something or someone

10. TISNSSI = 10. INSISTS
Refuses to yield

11. TIGVUEIF = 11. FUGITIVE
Person running away from the law

12. SOIFLS = 12. FOSSIL
Skeleton or imprint of an organism in a rock

13. EDLYDAE = 13. DELAYED
Put off until another time

14. GYOGS = 14. SOGGY
Soaked with moisture

15. NITGVEIIOSATN = 15. INVESTIGATION
Systematic examination

Holes Vocabulary Juggle Letters 2

1. IOATR = 1. _____
   Relation between two things

2. TMLAEEITIG = 2. _____
   Lawful; legal

3. PESBELAICD = 3. _____
   Vile; awful

4. HRSKNA = 4. _____
   Got smaller

5. NCIGTHHI = 5. _____
   Hooking to; connecting

6. LSUDANI = 6. _____
   Instrument that indicates local solar time

7. MECDHRNEOP = 7. _____
   Understand

8. EHTEADXSU = 8. _____
   Very tired; weary

9. LGLUY = 9. _____
   Deep ditch cut in the earth by running water

10. SSRPEOEUPOTR = 10. _____
    Absurd; ridiculous

11. GSYOG = 11. _____
    Soaked with moisture

12. ETNRMOT = 12. _____
    Great pain or anguish

13. IOFSLS = 13. _____
    Skeleton or imprint of an organism in a rock

14. AEDRD = 14. _____
    Anticipate with fear, alarm, or reluctance

15. INMQESREEUTR = 15. _____
    Necessary things

Holes Vocabulary Juggle Letters 2 Answer Key

1. IOATR = 1. RATIO
Relation between two things

2. TMLAEEITIG = 2. LEGITIMATE
Lawful; legal

3. PESBELAICD = 3. DESPICABLE
Vile; awful

4. HRSKNA = 4. SHRANK
Got smaller

5. NCIGTHHI = 5. HITCHING
Hooking to; connecting

6. LSUDANI = 6. SUNDIAL
Instrument that indicates local solar time

7. MECDHRNEOP = 7. COMPREHEND
Understand

8. EHTEADXSU = 8. EXHAUSTED
Very tired; weary

9. LGLUY = 9. GULLY
Deep ditch cut in the earth by running water

10. SSRPEOEUPOTR = 10. PREPOSTEROUS
Absurd; ridiculous

11. GSYOG = 11. SOGGY
Soaked with moisture

12. ETNRMOT = 12. TORMENT
Great pain or anguish

13. IOFSLS = 13. FOSSIL
Skeleton or imprint of an organism in a rock

14. AEDRD = 14. DREAD
Anticipate with fear, alarm, or reluctance

15. INMQESREEUTR = 15. REQUIREMENTS
Necessary things

Holes Vocabulary Juggle Letters 3

1. SRSECU = 1. _____
   Appeals for evil or injury to befall someone or something

2. ICESPEDBAL = 2. _____
   Vile; awful

3. REIROSPUAC = 3. _____
   Dangerously lacking in security or stability

4. VASERERCNEPE = 4. _____
   Not giving up

5. AHRNKS = 5. _____
   Got smaller

6. AILTCEML = 6. _____
   Like or containing a metal

7. COPINSRO = 7. _____
   Spider-like animal with a venomous tail

8. UGRE = 8. _____
   Force moving one to do something

9. EOTPDERTC = 9. _____
   Keep safe; guarded

10. RHPENDOEMC = 10. _____
    Understand

11. LARDW = 11. _____
    Speech characterized by lengthened, drawn-out vowels

12. ADERCHP = 12. _____
    Very dry

13. SOCNTOONCIC = 13. _____
    Preparations made by mixing ingredients

14. YIFER = 14. _____
    Very hot; like fire

15. PCSUSTE = 15. _____
    Have doubts about; distrust

Holes Vocabulary Juggle Letters 3 Answer Key

1. SRSECU = 1. CURSES
Appeals for evil or injury to befall someone or something

2. ICESPEDBAL = 2. DESPICABLE
Vile; awful

3. REIROSPUAC = 3. PRECARIOUS
Dangerously lacking in security or stability

4. VASERERCNEPE = 4. PERSEVERANCE
Not giving up

5. AHRNKS = 5. SHRANK
Got smaller

6. AILTCEML = 6. METALLIC
Like or containing a metal

7. COPINSRO = 7. SCORPION
Spider-like animal with a venomous tail

8. UGRE = 8. URGE
Force moving one to do something

9. EOTPDERTC = 9. PROTECTED
Keep safe; guarded

10. RHPENDOEMC = 10. COMPREHEND
Understand

11. LARDW = 11. DRAWL
Speech characterized by lengthened, drawn-out vowels

12. ADERCHP = 12. PARCHED
Very dry

13. SOCNTOONCIC = 13. CONCOCTIONS
Preparations made by mixing ingredients

14. YIFER = 14. FIERY
Very hot; like fire

15. PCSUSTE = 15. SUSPECT
Have doubts about; distrust

Holes Vocabulary Juggle Letters 4

1. DETJAANC = 1. _____
   Close together; next to

2. ADNILSU = 2. _____
   Instrument that indicates local solar time

3. LCLEMTAI = 3. _____
   Like or containing a metal

4. NEMDCNDOE = 4. _____
   Found guilty

5. OTOL = 5. _____
   Stolen goods

6. IOREDISUL = 6. _____
   Mentally confused

7. CEUSPST = 7. _____
   Have doubts about; distrust

8. USITJICNDOIR = 8. _____
   Area of authority or control

9. EEDLAYD = 9. _____
   Put off until another time

10. EDRHPECMON = 10. _____
    Understand

11. GOIRTNHBB = 11. _____
    Beating rapidly or violently; pounding

12. UISYMETRSO = 12. _____
    Not fully understood

13. ADLASTNEW = 13. _____
    Uncultivated or desolate country

14. ERUEOQTSG = 14. _____
    Outlandish; bizarre

15. ACENTR = 15. _____
    Delicious, invigorating drink

Holes Vocabulary Juggle Letters 4 Answer Key

1. DETJAANC = 1. ADJACENT
Close together; next to

2. ADNILSU = 2. SUNDIAL
Instrument that indicates local solar time

3. LCLEMTAI = 3. METALLIC
Like or containing a metal

4. NEMDCNDOE = 4. CONDEMNED
Found guilty

5. OTOL = 5. LOOT
Stolen goods

6. IOREDISUL = 6. DELIRIOUS
Mentally confused

7. CEUSPST = 7. SUSPECT
Have doubts about; distrust

8. USITJICNDOIR = 8. JURISDICTION
Area of authority or control

9. EEDLAYD = 9. DELAYED
Put off until another time

10. EDRHPECMON = 10. COMPREHEND
Understand

11. GOIRTNHBB = 11. THROBBING
Beating rapidly or violently; pounding

12. UISYMETRSO = 12. MYSTERIOUS
Not fully understood

13. ADLASTNEW = 13. WASTELAND
Uncultivated or desolate country

14. ERUEOQTSG = 14. GROTESQUE
Outlandish; bizarre

15. ACENTR = 15. NECTAR
Delicious, invigorating drink

ADJACENT	Close together; next to
AMAZED	Filled with surprise; astonished
APPRECIATE	Value
AWKWARD	Clumsy; unskillful
BARREN	Sterile; dull; unfruitful
CALLUSED	Having a thickening and hardness of skin

CAUTIOUS	Careful
CERTAIN	Sure
COMPREHEND	Understand
CONCOCTIONS	Preparations made by mixing ingredients
CONDEMNED	Found guilty
CURSES	Appeals for evil or injury to befall someone or something

DEFECTIVE	Flawed; doesn't work right
DELAYED	Put off until another time
DELIRIOUS	Mentally confused
DESCENDANTS	Individuals from which others come; opposite of ancestors
DESOLATE	Dreary; unfit for habitation or use
DESPICABLE	Vile; awful

DOOMED	Condemned to a severe penalty
DRAWL	Speech characterized by lengthened, drawn-out vowels
DREAD	Anticipate with fear, alarm, or reluctance
ENGRAVED	Carved, cut, or etched into something
EVAPORATED	Changed to vapor
EXHAUSTED	Very tired; weary

FABULOUS	Barely believable; astonishing; amazing
FAMILIAR	Often encountered; known
FEEBLE	Lacking strength
FIERY	Very hot; like fire
FLINCH	Draw away from something surprising or painful
FOSSIL	Skeleton or imprint of an organism in a rock

FUGITIVE	Person running away from the law
GROTESQUE	Outlandish; bizarre
GULLY	Deep ditch cut in the earth by running water
HAZE	Moisture, dust, or vapor suspended in the air
HITCHING	Hooking to; connecting
HOVER	Floating or suspended in air

HUMILIATING	Embarrassing; being disgraced
IMAGE	Reproduction of the form of something or someone
IMPROVE	Get better
INCARCERATED	Shut in; confined--usually in jail
INEXPLICABLE	Not able to be explained or interpreted
INGREDIENT	Something that is an element; a part of

INSISTS	Refuses to yield
INVESTIGATION	Systematic examination
JURISDICTION	Area of authority or control
LEGITIMATE	Lawful; legal
LOGICAL	Consistent in reasoning
LOOT	Stolen goods

LOPSIDED	Heavier or larger on one side than the other
METALLIC	Like or containing a metal
MIRAGE	An illusion; something deceptive
MYSTERIOUS	Not fully understood
NECTAR	Delicious, invigorating drink
PARCHED	Very dry

PERSEVERANCE	Not giving up
PIG	Jargon formed by putting first consonant at the end of a word and adding a syllable: ___ Latin
PRECARIOUS	Dangerously lacking in security or stability
PRECIPICE	Extremely steep or overhanging mass of rock
PREPOSTEROUS	Absurd; ridiculous
PROTECTED	Keep safe; guarded

PROTRUDING	Sticking out; jutting out
RATIO	Relation between two things
REFUGE	Place of protection or shelter
REQUIREMENTS	Necessary things
RETRIEVED	Got back; regained
SCARCITY	Shortage

SCORPION	Spider-like animal with a venomous tail
SHRANK	Got smaller
SOGGY	Soaked with moisture
SPEWED	Forced out
SPRAWLED	Spread out in straggling or disorderly fashion
STATIONERY	Writing paper and envelopes

STIFLING	Smothering; suffocating
SUBTLE	So slight as to be difficult to distinguish
SUNDIAL	Instrument that indicates local solar time
SUSPECT	Have doubts about; distrust
SWISH	Move with a whistle or hiss
TEDIOUS	Tiresome; wearisome

THROBBING	Beating rapidly or violently; pounding
TORMENT	Great pain or anguish
URGE	Force moving one to do something
VENOM	Poisonous secretion of an animal, such as a spider or snake
VENTILATION	Admitting fresh air to replace stale air
VISIBLE	Able to be seen

WASTELAND	Uncultivated or desolate country
WHEELBARROW	Vehicle with handles & a wheel used to convey loads by hand
WRITHED	Twisted; squirmed

Holes Vocabulary

AMAZED	STATIONERY	SUBTLE	DESOLATE	JURISDICTION
NECTAR	SWISH	REFUGE	IMAGE	CONCOCTIONS
RATIO	APPRECIATE	FREE SPACE	DELAYED	GULLY
SPEWED	LOGICAL	VENOM	FUGITIVE	REQUIREMENTS
DESCENDANTS	SOGGY	CURSES	COMPREHEND	PROTRUDING

Holes Vocabulary

STIFLING	LOOT	FLINCH	SCARCITY	RETRIEVED
IMPROVE	PRECIPICE	CERTAIN	DEFECTIVE	INGREDIENT
WRITHED	WASTELAND	FREE SPACE	PARCHED	CONDEMNED
SPRAWLED	METALLIC	CAUTIOUS	CALLUSED	VISIBLE
EXHAUSTED	DREAD	PREPOSTEROUS	HUMILIATING	FABULOUS

Holes Vocabulary

DRAWL	INVESTIGATION	DEFECTIVE	SUBTLE	BARREN
PROTECTED	LEGITIMATE	SUNDIAL	DELIRIOUS	FAMILIAR
DESPICABLE	AMAZED	FREE SPACE	DESCENDANTS	LOOT
EVAPORATED	SUSPECT	SCORPION	URGE	REQUIREMENTS
TORMENT	PREPOSTEROUS	METALLIC	ENGRAVED	HAZE

Holes Vocabulary

IMAGE	CURSES	CERTAIN	FUGITIVE	RATIO
TEDIOUS	FEEBLE	GROTESQUE	INGREDIENT	JURISDICTION
PRECIPICE	SPEWED	FREE SPACE	PRECARIOUS	IMPROVE
WASTELAND	EXHAUSTED	HOVER	GULLY	CONDEMNED
SHRANK	AWKWARD	CAUTIOUS	INEXPLICABLE	SPRAWLED

Holes Vocabulary

TEDIOUS	INSISTS	VENOM	CALLUSED	MIRAGE
DOOMED	PROTRUDING	HUMILIATING	SUSPECT	CAUTIOUS
SOGGY	WHEELBARROW	FREE SPACE	SHRANK	PRECARIOUS
SPRAWLED	ADJACENT	DESOLATE	INCARCERATED	NECTAR
APPRECIATE	CONDEMNED	HITCHING	TORMENT	DREAD

Holes Vocabulary

SUBTLE	FLINCH	FEEBLE	FUGITIVE	RATIO
DESPICABLE	LEGITIMATE	PREPOSTEROUS	LOGICAL	DEFECTIVE
ENGRAVED	IMPROVE	FREE SPACE	GROTESQUE	DESCENDANTS
FOSSIL	EXHAUSTED	DRAWL	GULLY	IMAGE
MYSTERIOUS	CERTAIN	LOPSIDED	SPEWED	SCORPION

Holes Vocabulary

ADJACENT	PREPOSTEROUS	VISIBLE	SOGGY	PARCHED
SCORPION	SPRAWLED	WASTELAND	VENOM	REQUIREMENTS
INSISTS	TEDIOUS	FREE SPACE	MIRAGE	RETRIEVED
LOOT	CAUTIOUS	PRECARIOUS	IMPROVE	HOVER
STATIONERY	SPEWED	CURSES	DESPICABLE	DELIRIOUS

Holes Vocabulary

DOOMED	AWKWARD	CONCOCTIONS	DESOLATE	PROTECTED
DREAD	DRAWL	DELAYED	HUMILIATING	INVESTIGATION
HITCHING	CERTAIN	FREE SPACE	EXHAUSTED	INEXPLICABLE
ENGRAVED	SUBTLE	FAMILIAR	FLINCH	PERSEVERANCE
AMAZED	STIFLING	GROTESQUE	MYSTERIOUS	JURISDICTION

Holes Vocabulary

APPRECIATE	CAUTIOUS	PROTECTED	HAZE	WRITHED
DEFECTIVE	SUSPECT	AWKWARD	COMPREHEND	PRECARIOUS
FAMILIAR	ADJACENT	FREE SPACE	INGREDIENT	GROTESQUE
RETRIEVED	LOPSIDED	BARREN	HUMILIATING	VISIBLE
DESCENDANTS	PIG	EVAPORATED	EXHAUSTED	CONCOCTIONS

Holes Vocabulary

MIRAGE	REFUGE	SWISH	URGE	WASTELAND
FIERY	DESOLATE	RATIO	CONDEMNED	STATIONERY
FLINCH	FOSSIL	FREE SPACE	NECTAR	SCORPION
VENOM	INEXPLICABLE	SPRAWLED	SOGGY	TEDIOUS
INCARCERATED	THROBBING	DELIRIOUS	MYSTERIOUS	SUNDIAL

Holes Vocabulary

PERSEVERANCE	RATIO	NECTAR	MYSTERIOUS	VENOM
SCORPION	DESCENDANTS	STATIONERY	WASTELAND	ENGRAVED
SOGGY	JURISDICTION	FREE SPACE	VISIBLE	DELAYED
FIERY	DESPICABLE	AMAZED	DOOMED	INGREDIENT
REFUGE	DREAD	PARCHED	FLINCH	AWKWARD

Holes Vocabulary

INCARCERATED	GROTESQUE	LOPSIDED	EVAPORATED	LOOT
SPEWED	CAUTIOUS	HOVER	FOSSIL	SWISH
DESOLATE	DELIRIOUS	FREE SPACE	CURSES	HUMILIATING
TORMENT	CERTAIN	WHEELBARROW	CONDEMNED	PROTRUDING
LEGITIMATE	PREPOSTEROUS	INSISTS	PRECARIOUS	INEXPLICABLE

Holes Vocabulary

FABULOUS	SUNDIAL	INVESTIGATION	FEEBLE	PRECIPICE
DOOMED	DEFECTIVE	JURISDICTION	HITCHING	VENOM
REFUGE	DESPICABLE	FREE SPACE	RETRIEVED	FIERY
VENTILATION	TEDIOUS	DESCENDANTS	THROBBING	SUSPECT
DREAD	MIRAGE	SCARCITY	INSISTS	VISIBLE

Holes Vocabulary

FOSSIL	SWISH	WASTELAND	INCARCERATED	WRITHED
CAUTIOUS	PREPOSTEROUS	GROTESQUE	PIG	FUGITIVE
LEGITIMATE	CURSES	FREE SPACE	IMAGE	ENGRAVED
AMAZED	ADJACENT	SHRANK	WHEELBARROW	STATIONERY
PERSEVERANCE	RATIO	DELAYED	DRAWL	LOPSIDED

Holes Vocabulary

NECTAR	CONDEMNED	INVESTIGATION	TORMENT	MIRAGE
DESPICABLE	CURSES	EVAPORATED	DESOLATE	SUNDIAL
REQUIREMENTS	COMPREHEND	FREE SPACE	PRECARIOUS	CONCOCTIONS
VISIBLE	DEFECTIVE	SHRANK	DOOMED	HOVER
FABULOUS	LOPSIDED	URGE	GROTESQUE	DRAWL

Holes Vocabulary

PREPOSTEROUS	INEXPLICABLE	FOSSIL	FEEBLE	HITCHING
CERTAIN	HUMILIATING	INCARCERATED	FAMILIAR	DREAD
IMAGE	BARREN	FREE SPACE	APPRECIATE	WRITHED
FUGITIVE	TEDIOUS	STATIONERY	METALLIC	MYSTERIOUS
PRECIPICE	ADJACENT	RATIO	SPEWED	CALLUSED

Holes Vocabulary

DESOLATE	COMPREHEND	WRITHED	APPRECIATE	VENOM
LOPSIDED	THROBBING	EXHAUSTED	GROTESQUE	SCORPION
FUGITIVE	PERSEVERANCE	FREE SPACE	DEFECTIVE	STIFLING
INGREDIENT	WASTELAND	METALLIC	INSISTS	AMAZED
REQUIREMENTS	CONCOCTIONS	TORMENT	EVAPORATED	CERTAIN

Holes Vocabulary

REFUGE	LOGICAL	STATIONERY	SPRAWLED	ENGRAVED
IMPROVE	DREAD	GULLY	DELIRIOUS	INVESTIGATION
FABULOUS	SCARCITY	FREE SPACE	SOGGY	AWKWARD
PRECIPICE	PARCHED	MIRAGE	PIG	DOOMED
NECTAR	VENTILATION	CURSES	DRAWL	WHEELBARROW

Holes Vocabulary

FIERY	METALLIC	EXHAUSTED	SWISH	DESOLATE
CERTAIN	PRECIPICE	TORMENT	VENOM	FAMILIAR
INGREDIENT	SPRAWLED	FREE SPACE	PRECARIOUS	FEEBLE
INSISTS	INCARCERATED	DESCENDANTS	IMAGE	DOOMED
CALLUSED	SUSPECT	SUNDIAL	STIFLING	DELIRIOUS

Holes Vocabulary

CURSES	FOSSIL	INEXPLICABLE	WASTELAND	THROBBING
PERSEVERANCE	AWKWARD	RATIO	HAZE	PARCHED
LOPSIDED	MIRAGE	FREE SPACE	SCARCITY	REQUIREMENTS
VENTILATION	BARREN	SCORPION	GULLY	DRAWL
LOOT	LOGICAL	DELAYED	JURISDICTION	SUBTLE

Holes Vocabulary

GROTESQUE	LOPSIDED	SOGGY	TORMENT	SWISH
DELAYED	PROTRUDING	FABULOUS	PROTECTED	FEEBLE
SCARCITY	LOGICAL	FREE SPACE	APPRECIATE	HITCHING
HUMILIATING	CALLUSED	CAUTIOUS	PREPOSTEROUS	AMAZED
DESOLATE	DOOMED	EXHAUSTED	THROBBING	FAMILIAR

Holes Vocabulary

DRAWL	ENGRAVED	INSISTS	INVESTIGATION	BARREN
DESPICABLE	PRECIPICE	JURISDICTION	STATIONERY	TEDIOUS
PARCHED	CERTAIN	FREE SPACE	SCORPION	WASTELAND
CONCOCTIONS	DREAD	SUSPECT	INEXPLICABLE	PIG
EVAPORATED	LEGITIMATE	DELIRIOUS	FIERY	PERSEVERANCE

Holes Vocabulary

PROTECTED	PROTRUDING	GULLY	CERTAIN	DELAYED
DESCENDANTS	MYSTERIOUS	SCORPION	ENGRAVED	METALLIC
APPRECIATE	SHRANK	FREE SPACE	CALLUSED	VENTILATION
CAUTIOUS	LOGICAL	DOOMED	DRAWL	THROBBING
SOGGY	EXHAUSTED	IMAGE	EVAPORATED	HOVER

Holes Vocabulary

LOPSIDED	URGE	SUBTLE	WHEELBARROW	SPEWED
FEEBLE	STATIONERY	IMPROVE	DEFECTIVE	HITCHING
DREAD	DESOLATE	FREE SPACE	MIRAGE	ADJACENT
CURSES	INCARCERATED	NECTAR	RATIO	VENOM
INGREDIENT	INEXPLICABLE	DELIRIOUS	SCARCITY	REFUGE

Holes Vocabulary

SWISH	DRAWL	MIRAGE	FABULOUS	PREPOSTEROUS
PARCHED	PRECIPICE	PROTRUDING	LOPSIDED	SPEWED
REQUIREMENTS	LOOT	FREE SPACE	IMPROVE	VENOM
ENGRAVED	METALLIC	THROBBING	WHEELBARROW	AWKWARD
SUSPECT	DESOLATE	SCORPION	DOOMED	DEFECTIVE

Holes Vocabulary

INVESTIGATION	SCARCITY	FLINCH	STATIONERY	CALLUSED
FUGITIVE	DELAYED	TORMENT	CONCOCTIONS	COMPREHEND
HOVER	GULLY	FREE SPACE	PERSEVERANCE	SHRANK
IMAGE	ADJACENT	INCARCERATED	AMAZED	PRECARIOUS
DESCENDANTS	VISIBLE	FIERY	CAUTIOUS	INSISTS

Holes Vocabulary

PIG	DESOLATE	SCORPION	VENTILATION	LOOT
GROTESQUE	SWISH	URGE	PRECARIOUS	DESPICABLE
RATIO	FAMILIAR	FREE SPACE	FABULOUS	PRECIPICE
DEFECTIVE	DELIRIOUS	FEEBLE	CAUTIOUS	FLINCH
ADJACENT	STATIONERY	DREAD	LOGICAL	WASTELAND

Holes Vocabulary

PARCHED	THROBBING	DESCENDANTS	GULLY	INCARCERATED
FIERY	HOVER	CURSES	IMPROVE	SCARCITY
MIRAGE	PERSEVERANCE	FREE SPACE	STIFLING	INSISTS
SOGGY	VENOM	FUGITIVE	DOOMED	VISIBLE
PROTRUDING	AWKWARD	EVAPORATED	NECTAR	INGREDIENT

Holes Vocabulary

DRAWL	SPEWED	PARCHED	DEFECTIVE	LOOT
ADJACENT	SPRAWLED	LOPSIDED	SCARCITY	INSISTS
FABULOUS	PREPOSTEROUS	FREE SPACE	IMAGE	IMPROVE
DREAD	HITCHING	FAMILIAR	REFUGE	INEXPLICABLE
NECTAR	HAZE	VENTILATION	LOGICAL	RETRIEVED

Holes Vocabulary

REQUIREMENTS	ENGRAVED	EVAPORATED	APPRECIATE	SUNDIAL
DESPICABLE	HUMILIATING	INCARCERATED	METALLIC	RATIO
PERSEVERANCE	GULLY	FREE SPACE	STATIONERY	DESOLATE
PIG	VENOM	DESCENDANTS	TORMENT	HOVER
CAUTIOUS	PRECARIOUS	DELAYED	FLINCH	BARREN

Holes Vocabulary

HITCHING	SHRANK	SUBTLE	STATIONERY	INEXPLICABLE
DESPICABLE	CAUTIOUS	URGE	PROTECTED	EVAPORATED
DELAYED	FUGITIVE	FREE SPACE	PARCHED	FLINCH
LOOT	STIFLING	VENTILATION	WASTELAND	NECTAR
JURISDICTION	FABULOUS	REFUGE	DOOMED	PRECIPICE

Holes Vocabulary

LEGITIMATE	LOGICAL	MIRAGE	GROTESQUE	APPRECIATE
DESOLATE	INGREDIENT	FAMILIAR	SWISH	TORMENT
VISIBLE	FOSSIL	FREE SPACE	INSISTS	COMPREHEND
IMAGE	DRAWL	DREAD	SUSPECT	SCORPION
ADJACENT	SCARCITY	EXHAUSTED	LOPSIDED	HAZE

www.ingramcontent.com/pod-product-compliance
Lightning Source LLC
Chambersburg PA
CBHW080444090526
44586CB00047B/2326